MW00700766

"There is no way to prepare for the wonder and tranquility of life at the [T...] the forest paths, the whisper of pine sough, the vigilance of eagles in the [...] gifts of the very special family who have come to be the stewards of this [...] once respectful of rare wilderness and attentive to the refinements and culinary knowledge of the old world. Their oysters come from the next cove, their salmon from a family of fishermen on Kachemak Bay, the vegetables and herbs from their own gardens. This is local food, harvested for the table by highly skilled chefs who are themselves devoted to sustained living in the far north. Here, it is possible to restore the spirit to a sense of wonder: to slip by kayak through the still waters at dawn among otters and sea lions, to feel your heart leap with the fish. You will take home with you a memory of earth as it was and still is in such rare places, and once home, in your own kitchen, with the guidance of this book, you can bring a bit of this world to your own."

—CAROLYN FORCHÉ, Lannan Visiting Professor of Poetry and Professor of English at Georgetown University

"My daughter and I visited Tutka Bay four years ago and we have very, very fond memories of the experience; it's a truly magical place, made all the more so by the wonderfully warm welcome we received. Of all the places I've been in the course of my travels I think this may be the one that I find my mind returning most often, and this book takes me right back to that marvellous experience. The recipes are tantalising, the photographs breathtaking. Just reading the list of contents aloud transports me back to Tutka Bay in my imagination. I can't wait to try some of the recipes."

—JOANNE HARRIS, acclaimed British author of the award-winning novel CHOCOLAT

"Whenever I think of Kirsten Dixon and her beautiful Tutka Bay Lodge, I can't help but smile. It is a place infused with a sense of joy, discovery, and adventure—but after the bear viewing and whale watching, there is no greater treat than sitting down at her table and enjoying the deep simple deliciousness of Kirsten's cooking and her daughter Mandy's glorious baking. The recipes in this lovely book bring it all home, and we are the luckier for it."

—DANI SHAPIRO, author of SLOW MOTION AND DEVOTION

"I loved my stay at Tutka Bay Lodge. A breathtaking location, the warmest hospitality, and exceptional food. Now Kirsten and Mandy are revealing a few of those secret recipes."

—DAVID VANN, internationally best-selling author

"As a writer, as soon as I read Kirsten Dixon's tender instructions for the crab omelette, to fold the omelette over like a letter, I read the recipe twice and knew that letter was for me! And I wanted to read the whole book and eat the covers.

"Tutka Bay is a magical place and its vivid spirit touches every dish in this delicious volume."

—RON CARLSON, award-winning novelist

"Tutka Bay is magic. The natural beauty of the place is (almost) enough to fulfill every sense. But then there's Kirsten Dixon's food. Every meal—from the morning muffins, breads and egg dishes to the salads and sandwiches to the wild salmon and halibut and crab at dinner—struck the perfect note. This is a collection of recipes that will appeal to every cook— those that have shared her home in Alaska and those who just dream of being there. The Tutka Bay Summer Paella—chock-full of Alaska's best seafood—is a dish I will never forget. So happy to have this collection of recipes from such a talented chef and writer."

—KATHY GUNST, cookbook author, writer, blogger, and Resident Chef for WBUR's Here and Now

"This is a beautiful book full of photographs and recipes from an enchanted land that few will have the chance to visit . . . how lucky for us that Kirsten and Mandy have taken the time to share their story. Reading this book is like having a seat at the Chef's Table . . . prepare to be inspired!"

—STEPHEN DURFEE, Pastry chef, Chef Instructor at the CIA Greystone, Chocolatier

FODOR'S BEST HOTELS IN THE WORLD AWARD 2012:

"The mere fact that this remote, six-cabin Alaskan getaway—situated on a 7-mile-long fjord—is accessible only by boat is a good indicator that there's no real reason to leave this magical spot. Unless it's for an off-site excursion, that is. Start the day with morning yoga, then choose from daily activities such as a visit to a local oyster farm, cooking classes aboard a converted crabbing boat, or a helicopter ride to explore an active glacier. Later, relax on the new bayside deck, swap stories with other guests at the nightly wine-and-cheese reception, and enjoy dinner prepared by the resort's co-owner, celebrated chef Kirsten Dixon."

FOOD AND WINE MAGAZINE:

"To reach Tutka Bay Lodge, we boarded a small boat that took us from the little village of Homer to a remote peninsula. Ozzie, a sea otter, greeted us at the dock; other regular guests include bald eagles, humpback whales and black bears. Once our boat puttered off, we were left standing in utter silence, staring out at the spruce-covered islands and down at the countless red and yellow and purple starfish beneath the surface of the clear water. But enough about the scenery: We came for the food . . . Tutka Bay Lodge co-owner Kirsten Dixon is perhaps the best-known chef in state."

COUNTRY LIVING:

"A talented chef, Kirsten regales us with culinary treasures that pay tribute to Alaska's rich bounty."

the
TUTKA BAY LODGE
COOKBOOK

Coastal Cuisine from the Wilds of Alaska

WITH KIRSTEN DIXON AND MANDY DIXON

FOOD PHOTOGRAPHY BY TYRONE POTGIETER

ALASKA
NORTHWEST
BOOKS®

Text © 2014 by Kirsten Dixon and Mandy Dixon
All photographs © 2014 by Tyrone Potgieter
except for the following: Front cover, top photo;
pages 12, 13, 17, 20, 21 (top right, middle right,
bottom middle, bottom right), 22, 62 (bottom), 70,
75, 95, 101, 107, 114, 116, 120, 136 (middle right),
146, 147, 162, 172, 173, 175, 178, 190 (top left,
bottom center), 206 (middle right, bottom left,
bottom center), 217 (bottom right) © Jeff Schultz.

All rights reserved. No part of this book may
be reproduced or transmitted in any form or by
any means, electronic or mechanical, including
photocopying, recording, or by any information
storage and retrieval system, without written
permission of the publisher.

Library of Congress Cataloging-in-Publication Data
Dixon, Kirsten.
  The Tutka Bay Lodge cookbook : coastal cuisine
from the wilds of Alaska / with Kirsten Dixon and
Mandy Dixon ; photography by Tyrone Potgieter.
    pages cm
  Includes index.
  ISBN 978-1-941821-82-4 (pbk.)
  ISBN 978-1-941821-15-2 (hardcover)
  ISBN 978-1-941821-14-5 (e-book)

  1. Cooking, American—Pacific Northwest style. 2.
Cooking—Alaska. 3. Tutka Bay Lodge (Alaska) I.
Dixon, Mandy. II. Title.
  TX715.2.P32D58 2014
  641.59798—dc23

Cartographer: Gray Mouse Graphics
Original design concept by Sini Salminen
Layout by Vicki Knapton

Published by Alaska Northwest Books®
An imprint of

GRAPHIC ARTS
BOOKS®

P.O. Box 56118
Portland, Oregon 97238-6118
503-254-5591
www.graphicartsbooks.com

Printed in China

To our mother and grandmother
Peggy Ford Schmidt, who has always
shown us how to live a life of adventure
with creativity and grace.

Contents

WE LOOK FOR SEASHELLS IN THE MORNING

LET'S TAKE OUR LUNCHEON BY THE SEA

EVERY COLOR OF SILVER

Red roof. Green spruce. Mercuried sheen on the surface of the water. Razor peaks dalmationed with snow.

A fluorescent orange jellyfish as big as a medium pizza pulses past under the boardwalk, trailing tentacles as long as your arm. Walk the boardwalk to the sundeck, or in this case, the one-million-shades-of-silver-in-the-sky deck, to discover flower baskets and handmade wooden rockers and a hot tub under a cupola. The deck is enormous, big enough to hold a square dance, or a touch football game, or an inauguration, or to sit in one of those rockers for the rest of your life and watch the light change on the water, breathing the fresh sprucey air. But the tour continues: the sauna, the vegetable garden, the greenhouse, the cabins, the Widgeon, and the lodge.

Welcome to the place beyond the end of the road, where the only way in is by boat from Homer and the only way out is against all your better judgment, because who wouldn't want to stay here in this paradise of sea and sky. Who wouldn't want to sit on the deck and watch the fledgling eagles tumble out of the giant spruce, knowing that whatever time it is, it is only a few hours until you are going to eat again: crab cakes benedict or Kachemak Bay seafood chowder or halibut with rhubarb and ginger. These are plates of food so artful, so visually pleasing—even the homemade butter with its bracelet of thyme leaves and flakes of coarse sea salt—and still you won't be prepared for the radical deliciousness.

None of this food has any business being this far into any wilderness, let alone roadless Alaska, and yet there is it again, on the end of your fork and on its way to your mouth.

You know how fresh air makes food taste better, how, when you have been backpacking all day even freeze-dried chicken stew tastes delicious? This isn't like that. Or if it is, it is like that to the two hundred and twenty seven millionth power.

Years of culinary school, a long apprenticeship under the most famous chef in America, unimaginable hard work, mind bending logistics—you don't just run down to the store here to buy Asian spices for the halibut shawarma or Comté cheese for the toasted barley risotto—and still, there is something extra in every plate of food that Kirsten and Mandy Dixon put on the table. Call it magic, call it love, call it an off-the-charts commitment to excellence, call it an addiction to the looks on the faces of the guests when they take the first surprising and deeply pleasing bite, there is an X factor at the Tutka Bay table that makes dining here an experience that can not be duplicated anywhere in the world.

Tutka Bay magic begins in the kitchen, but because the Dixons are who they are, they let it radiate out, to their employees, their guests, to all of Alaska. You might think community doesn't matter when you live nine miles across the water from the end of the road, but they would tell you it matters in that case all the more. Community conscious decisions are in every corner of this lodge, from the locally sourced food to the hand-thrown serving dishes to the giant driftwood chandeliers (weighing 125 pounds each) that hang over the massive dining table in the *Widgeon*—a ninety-foot troop transport boat beached on one end of the property—that now houses Mandy and Kirsten's cooking school.

This weekend I am very lucky, because the Dixon's community has enlarged itself to include me.

I am here to lead a three-day creative writing workshop for twenty-five Alaskans who have all paid an amount that cannot possibly cover costs to be here. I would quite happily clean toilets or hammer nails or wash dishes for the chance to spend one night in this paradise but what I get to do instead is set up shop in the *Widgeon* and do what I love most: talk about making stories.

The *Widgeon* has a few stories of its own to tell, converted once to carry herring, then crabs, then dragged onto land and enclosed with wooden planks to form a long and skinny and somewhat hulking two-story living space. Leave it to the Dixon women to bring their design expertise to the inside of this behemoth to make it rugged, stylish, and cozy—think Quasimodo with a heart of gold. And because good writing is one more thing on the long list of things the Dixon's believe in, this weekend, the *Widgeon* is ours.

From the moment we step off our water taxi from Homer, we are taken in, taken care of, fed like queens, fed like the luckiest people to happen upon food in the history of Alaska travel. We are taken out, to kayak among the islands of Kachemak Bay, where we cross paths with a mother otter and her raft of babies, see orca spouts in the distance, and farther, across Lower Cook Inlet, the snow-covered peaks of Iliamna, centerpiece of the Chigmit Mountains. We are taken hiking, along the driftwood-strewn beaches and the fireweed filled meadows, through rain forest filled with ferns and leaves the size of a man's torso, through old-growth trees too big to put our arms around.

In the early morning I sit out on the big deck, watching, listening. Every time the sun breaks through the clouds, those long northern rays supersaturating the blue hull of a boat, the yellow arm of a jacket, the cheerful red roofs of the lodge, I gasp. When it retreats, making all surfaces reflective, making the sky and the bay merge into one entity, I gasp again.

On the other side of the inlet a bald eagle dives for a fish and connects. But the fish is so large the eagle can't lift himself and it out of the water, so he slalom skis it over to the beach and hurls it onto the gray stones and broken shells, shakes his wings and tail feathers as if restoring his dignity, and prepares to dig into breakfast.

I admire his technique, but do not envy him. Kirsten and Mandy are in the kitchen. Who knows what's in store for me today.

—Pam Houston

WITH GRATITUDE

I am constantly amazed and proud of my hard-working, close-knit family who pull together to often accomplish the nearly impossible.

Every summer, Tutka Bay Lodge guests experience the hard work and commitment of my two daughters, Carly and Mandy. Each brings something different to the Tutka Bay table but we couldn't be who we are without them.

Mandy, a skilled and talented pastry chef, works with me on many culinary projects. She helps to train new chefs in the kitchens of our lodges, and travels often with me when we teach cooking classes. When I whimsically want to cook salmon burgers at a music festival, or when I want to open a little café along the harbor in Homer, or when I want to write a new cookbook, Mandy never flinches in her partnership and commitment to our creative, but sometimes intense and challenging, projects. Mandy crafted and designed all the recipes in this collection, she prepared all of them in testing, and she styled each dish that was photographed. She did all the heavy lifting for this project.

Carly has guided me in thinking about our wellness program at the lodge. We offer massage, yoga, and other mind—body aesthetics that wouldn't be considered without her direction and contribution. Carly has a keen eye for the smallest of details—from how the table is set to the music playing in the background.

My son-in-law, Tyrone Potgieter, has taken most of the photos in this cookbook collection, as well as our previous cookbook, *The Winterlake Lodge Cookbook*. His remarkable creative talent—for building, for fishing, for piloting, and for photography, has enriched our family and has been a contribution to our lodge life.

Mandy's longtime boyfriend, Neil Lippincott, has worked for us as our Anchorage-based expeditor for the past eight years since my father, Jim, retired from that very same position. In the summertime, Neil is constantly driving supplies down to Homer and loading boats heading over to the lodge. Neil works closely with Carl in the winter on many of our building projects.

And, of course, I am grateful for my husband, Carl, who continues to be the center and strength of our family. Carl inspires and guides us every day to work hard, to respect the natural world, and to be kind and good to others.

Beyond our family, a special thanks to guide manager Michael Gustafson who has been with us from the beginning of our new lodge adventure. And, to photographer and friend Jeff Schultz who contributed images to this collection.

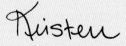

WELCOME TO TUTKA BAY LODGE

There is so much that is old-world about how our family lives in Alaska. We own and operate two backcountry lodges and we've done this work nearly all of our adult lives. My husband, Carl, and I, our daughters, Carly and Mandy, and the new additions of our son-in-law, Tyrone, our grandson, Rohnen, and Mandy's boyfriend, Neil, all work together to craft a life, a lifestyle, that centers around three themes: the natural world, our culinary lives, and living a life of adventure.

Mandy and I are both trained chefs. We learned to cook in the classic French style in terms of how we prepare much of our food and how we view our work. We take our kitchens seriously. As in the French style, our company is a family-managed affair. Carl and I even live above the kitchens at both of our lodges, a decidedly old-fashioned thing to do.

Carl and Ty oversee the outdoor program, offering at times life-changing and remarkable adventures to our guests. Carly is trained in yoga and massage and she crafts our wellness programs as well as offers her management expertise. Rohnen, at the tender age of two, has already begun to identify and replicate bird sounds. Mandy manages and trains the culinary teams at both lodges and she oversees our small La Baleine Café on the Homer Spit. She also works closely with me on public events, culinary demonstrations, and developing menus and recipes. Neil expedites the gathering, shipping, and delivery of all our supplies including food, fuel, and building materials. Our entire family dedicate ourselves to our work, which is to share with guests the wildness we live so close to, our food and wine, and the daily adventure that living in Alaska brings us.

In our kitchen, we offer simple rustic Alaska cuisine with the hope in mind to offer our friendship, communicate our passion, and bring comfort and delight to the table. Every cook is a product of her or his family traditions, where they've traveled, and what they have experienced in the world. And, so it is with us. Our cuisine most often represents something meaningful to us that we wish to share with and express to our guests. We always interpret our food memories within the context of our geography and the fresh and unique foods we find in Alaska.

This recipe collection represents our cuisine at Tutka Bay Lodge, our seaside lodge nestled within the curve of a quiet cove at the entrance to Tutka Bay, a deep seven-mile fjord in Kachemak Bay, Alaska.

We bought the property in 2009 in something of a perfect moment. The previous owners were retiring. For more than thirty years, our family has lived near the western edge of the Alaska Range that leads up to Mount McKinley, about two hundred miles from the ocean. We were always curious about maritime culture—and cuisine. After exploring several seaside communities, we settled on Tutka Bay.

During the first week we were living at Tutka Bay Lodge full-time, in May of 2009, Carl took a couple of guests for a little after-dinner cruise around the bay and the nearby Herring Islands. It was dusk, but not dark yet because of our extended summer daylight. Mandy and I were finishing the last of the dishes and closedown of the kitchen for the night. Carl, as he usually does, offered for us to ride along but we declined. That night, Carl's first journey out with guests in our new neighborhood, an entire pod of orca whales surrounded our boat. One whale rose out of the water and up to the edge of the boat, looking at Carl with as much curiosity as Carl looked back at him. A startled guest took a picture with his camera, which turned out to be exactly what Carl saw—one giant whale eye. Carl came back breathless with the story. And, it seems that with every trip Carl takes into Kachemak Bay, he returns animated with a new tale of adventure. We are lucky to live among sea mammals, shorebirds, and such a complex diversity of wildlife here at Tutka Bay Lodge.

Seafood is the star of our cuisine, as it should be. We certainly serve our share of ocean-caught salmon throughout the entire summer season the lodge is open. Halibut, cod, rockfish, shrimp, and crab also are served nearly daily. We are lucky enough to have good fish purveyors whom we count as personal friends.

We are never too far from the garden in our cooking and many of our recipes include fresh-picked herbs or vegetables that grow well in Alaska. It's important to me that my daughters, and now grandson, continue as gardeners and that we at least grow some part of our food each summer. Our recipes often reflect that which we can grow ourselves.

And, the wildness of it all! The wild berries, herbs, mushrooms, and sea vegetables inspire us to remember where on the Earth we live and how lucky we are.

Our recipes are purposefully simple and designed for the home cook. We tested all recipes on a home stove and photographed all dishes as they were prepared and in natural light. In our kitchen, much of what we choose to cook is organic and we work hard to select and procure local products. Rather than stating it throughout the recipe collection, we hope you might use organic and high-quality local products whenever possible.

I have to add a special note of thanks to my daughter Mandy. Although some of the dialogue in this book is in my personal voice and some shared, Mandy has been coauthor and contributor every step of the way—from first discussions of recipe selections on scraps of paper to plate design to recipe testing. This has been a true collaborative and collective process.

We both hope you enjoy this small glimpse into our culinary lives at Tutka Bay Lodge.

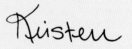

AWAY AND HOME AGAIN

It seems amazing to be standing here in the kitchen of my little café on the Homer Spit looking across the sunlit bay toward my family lodge in Tutka Bay. A few years ago, we were only distantly familiar with "ocean life," Kachemak Bay, and the small village of Homer. We had lived most of our lives in the interior, north of Anchorage, first along the Yentna River where I spent my earliest years at a fishing lodge, and then at Winterlake Lodge, further north and west at Mile 198 along the Iditarod Trail, where we moved when I was a teenager.

I was raised in Alaska backcountry lodges, which as anyone who shares that legacy knows, means plenty of long hours and hard work from an early age. Often my daily chores involved working in the garden, taking care of our menagerie of animals, and I particularly seemed to gravitate to the kitchen to help my mother (and sometimes to terrorize the chefs) when I was younger. Lucky for me, my mother taught me to cook as soon as I could reach the hardwood worktable that stood in the middle of our large country kitchen. Frequent early jobs assigned to me were to chop herbs and make endless varieties of cookie dough. My mother trained as a chef in France and emphasized proper technique from the very beginning. Today, that hardwood table sits in the center of our prep area in my café in Homer. In some ways, that old worktable is an icon of the culinary life I was born into.

When I was seventeen, I graduated from home-school and headed to culinary school. My mother always emphasized that culinary school didn't have to mean a lifelong commitment to cooking. It was a creative way to learn a good life skill and get used to life outside of rural Alaska. But, I never looked back or lost my enthusiasm for cooking.

I first went to the Cordon Bleu School in Pasadena and then on to the Culinary Institute of America (CIA) in St. Helena. Both schools taught me invaluable lessons but it was my years living in Napa that were formative in terms of who I am as a chef today.

At the CIA, Chef Stephen Durfee taught me how to look creatively at food and how to push the limits of what I could do. He taught me a love of baking and pastry arts, which I still have a preference for, although I cook both savory and sweet at the café and the lodges. Chef Durfee encouraged me to apply to work for the Thomas Keller Restaurant Group (TKRG) while I was still a student. I started first at Bouchon Bistro in Yountville, and then moved with Chef Dave Cruz to help open Ad Hoc just down the street. I continued to work and live in Napa after graduation, renting a small house near a vineyard in St. Helena and driving each day to Yountville.

Chef Thomas Keller, owner of both of these restaurants, taught me as well as all others who worked for him, to treat each other, our kitchens, our food, and our patrons with respect, dignity, and professionalism. Chef Keller's influence informed my commitment to quality and pride in my profession and influenced me in how our kitchens operate even today. Over the years, I've stayed in touch with many coworkers from those years and we've had several TKRG alumni work in our lodge kitchens. There's always a certain shared camaraderie we have knowing we will work our hardest and best together and we won't let each other down. I will always be deeply grateful to Chef Keller, Chef Cruz, and Chef Durfee and all the people I worked with in Napa for enriching my culinary life.

If the chefs of Napa and beyond have inspired and influenced me, the cuisine of my mother's kitchen and the lure of Alaska led me home. I eventually left California to return to my family business. Alaska is my home and I'm proud to be from such a unique and diversely rich place. Alaska offers me unexplored places, clean water and earth, wild salmon and other seafood, herbs and berries. It offers me a lifetime of opportunity to be creative and rustic and traditional all within the same dish. It offers me the opportunity to work closely and proudly with my family to run our own small business.

Since returning home, I have been able to travel often, as guest or visiting chef, and as student to learn about world cuisines. I've often traveled with my mother, whom I work closely with every day. We share a love of cooking, teaching, and learning about cuisine that makes our collaboration particularly rewarding. Sometimes we take different approaches to a similar dish but we enjoy the process of working through recipe and menu creation together.

This project is the second major recipe collection we've assembled as a team and we're already casually daydreaming about our next project together. But for now, our new adventures in Tutka Bay and Homer are captivating us and we are learning and sharing the culinary secrets of life lived along a beautiful ocean.

Mandy

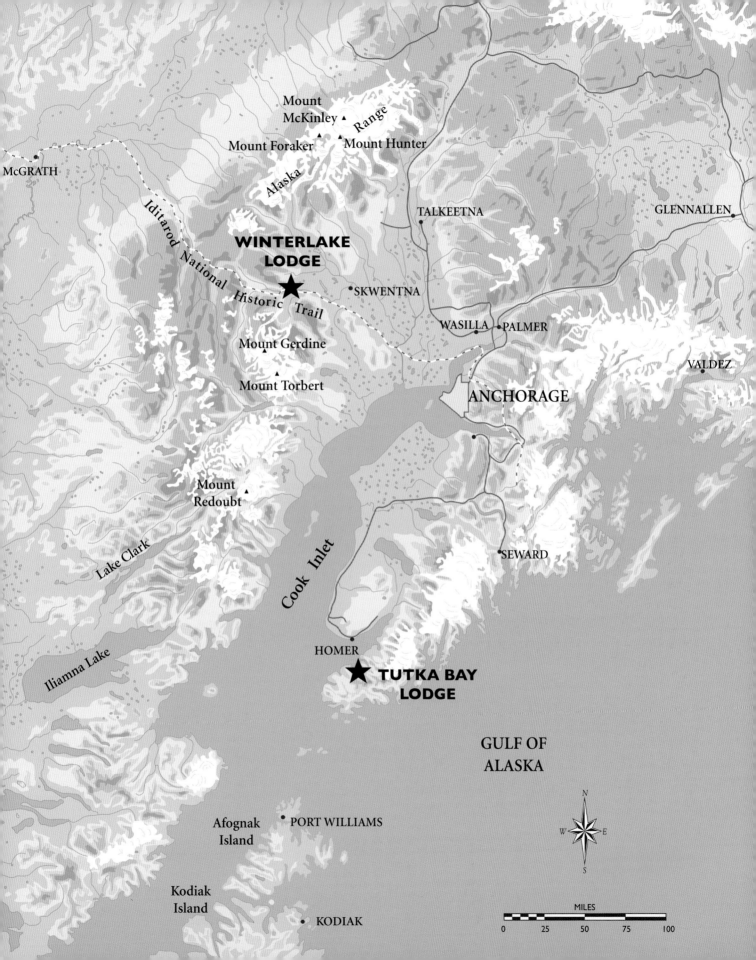

MORNING MEAL

At Tutka Bay Lodge, there are three collections of colors that matter the most. They are the daily changing hues of the blue sky that meets the rising green slope of Grace Ridge that then meets the steely water of the bay that we face and look toward from the lodge. It's as if this living landscape is a piece of fine art that we puzzle and ponder over. We don't think we could ever master, or tire of, the view from Tutka Bay Lodge toward the water. And, early morning is probably when we enjoy it the most.

The lodge slowly comes to life around 6:00 A.M. The chef is humming away in the kitchen and the first of many pots of freshly brewed coffee is underway. The lodge manager turns on the little brass lights in the main room and makes sure soft classical music is playing in the background. The breakfast table is set and the flowers are arranged. The setting is complete and waiting for the first breakfast guests to arrive.

On some mornings, guests head out early to go bear viewing along the Katmai Coast or fishing for halibut in the deep and productive waters of Kachemak Bay. We pack breakfasts to go, lunches to go, or both. The manager walks guests across the still-dewy deck and down the steel ramp to meet their boat captain for the twenty-five-minute trip to Homer. We like these departures, filled with the anticipation of the day and excitement of the adventure.

As guests migrate in to the main lodge and take their place for breakfast, discussions of the plans for the day buzz up and down our long communal table. Gus, our guide manager, is always nearby to answer any questions and to orchestrate daily adventure plans.

We serve gathered springwater at the table and freshly squeezed orange juice (we prefer Valencia oranges in the summer and navel oranges in the winter) in small glasses lined up neatly toward the top of woven placemats. Breadbaskets are filled with baked goods, and fruit is always on the table. Guests rarely know what a premium fresh fruit is in Alaska, as little is grown here.

Concerto for Violin and Strings in E, op. 8, no. 1, Antonio Vivaldi

Andante in C Major for Flute and Orchestra, K. 315, Wolfgang Amadeus Mozart

Sonata for Violin and Piano no. 5 in F major, Spring, op. 24:I Allegro, Ludwig van Beethoven

Pavane, op. 50, Gabriel Fauré

Concerto for Violin and Strings in G minor, op. 8, no. 2, R. 315, Antonio Vivaldi

Solomon HWV 67: The Arrival of the Queen of Sheba, George Frideric Handel

The Lark Ascending, Ralph Vaughan Williams.

It is important to us to have plenty of variety offered at the breakfast table. We like a mixture of quick and yeasted, fruited and savory breads on the table, and, at least in the present, we need to offer gluten-free options as well.

We make our own jams and jellies and Mandy can tell you I can hardly walk by a canning jar without wanting to fill it with something. Most of our jams are quick-style as they don't need to be shelved for very long. We rely on Alaska wild berries— blueberry, cranberry, salmonberry, red currants, as well as those from our garden—and on black currant, strawberry, raspberry, and others.

At breakfast, of course, egg cookery is often featured. We used to have our own chickens at Tutka Bay Lodge (Rhode Island Reds are my favorite layers), and I've had chickens at Winterlake Lodge, our other lodge along the Iditarod Trail, for many years, but recently we eliminated the extra "bear attraction" in lieu of sourcing quality organic local eggs from chickens raised outside of Homer.

So, what can we tell you about cooking eggs? There is such an abundance of information on the subject already. All we can offer in this collection is a few of our favorite breakfast dishes to remind you of them, to encourage you to try a dish in our way, and to consider our combination of seasonings and flavors.

Here are, however, a few bits of completely random egg cookery advice that we like to follow:

❧ *It's a bad idea to leave any part of the white uncooked— no one likes that.*

- *We add a splash of heavy cream into scrambled eggs. It keeps the eggs soft and tender.*

- *We cook omelets soft and turned in the French style. Stir eggs in a nonstick pan until they are mostly set, then bang the pan down to release the eggs from sticking to the bottom of the pan. Use a wide spatula to fold the omelet over like a letter.*

- *Our favorite herbs for simple egg dishes are (in order of preference) tarragon, basil, and thyme. We use fresh herbs all summer and dried herbs in the winter.*

- *We feel organic eggs are worth the extra money to avoid exposure to antibiotics.*

- *Good nonstick egg pans don't have to be expensive. It is better to get a new pan if the nonstick surface becomes scratched.*

- *We select 6-inch nonstick pans for fried eggs, 8-inch nonstick pans for omelets, and 12-inch nonstick pans for frittatas.*

- *Any vegetable added into eggs should already be cooked so moisture isn't released, which will make eggs soggy.*

At breakfast, we prefer to serve a meat platter separately from the main dish. We add in chicken sausage, thick bacon lacquered in maple or birch syrup, and hand-shaped sausage patties speckled with sage and pepper. Often we serve salmon bacon—cold-smoked bacon brushed with rhubarb simple syrup and heated up just until it is crisp.

We make seafood sausage with scraps trimmings of halibut, shrimp, and scallops, wrapped tightly in plastic wrap and poached in a shallow pan.

In the mornings, from the kitchen window, I can look out onto the edge of the world and water. I can often see guests and guides exploring the low tide areas in front of the lodge in the early morning, walking slowly to not disturb the animals underfoot. They gently lift up various colors and sizes of sea stars or anemones to show each other and search for small decorator crabs scurrying along the rocks. At extreme low tide, we walk along the rocks to gather sea lettuce and other edibles and hang them on to our "seaweed dryer" my son-in-law, Tyrone, built for me near the garden.

THE PERFECT CRAB OMELET

We were conflicted on whether to spell our crab omelet in the English style or omelette in the French style. In the end, although this is a French-style omelet, the eggs are all-American. Sometimes we add smoked paprika to our crab omelets.

3 LARGE EGGS

SALT AND FRESHLY GROUND
　BLACK PEPPER

1 TABLESPOON UNSALTED BUTTER

½ CUP PICKED DUNGENESS
　CRABMEAT

½ CUP MIXED HERBS
　(TARRAGON, CHIVES, CHERVIL
　ARE FAVORITES)

½ CUP SHREDDED GRUYÈRE CHEESE

Beat the eggs vigorously in a small mixing bowl, making sure the yolks and whites have blended well. Some people do this in a blender to get the eggs super aerated. Season with salt and pepper to taste.

Heat the butter in a hot medium nonstick sauté pan. When the butter has melted and bubbled up slightly, add in the egg mixture. Spread the mixture around the pan.

Shake the pan back and forth to keep the eggs moving and to slightly scramble them. When the eggs are about halfway cooked, tip them toward the farthest edge of the pan.

Add in the crabmeat and herbs along a centerline of the forming omelet. There will be some egg left on the bottom of the pan. Sprinkle on the cheese. Gently fold this bottom egg over the mass of the cooked egg and crab-herb mixture.

Rap the edge of the pan on the far end a couple of times onto a counter-top surface. This will move the egg into an oval shape. Turn the omelet out onto a plate. The perfect omelet won't have any darkened brown color on the outside.

Makes 1 omelet.

BREAKFAST RICE BOWL

We serve this dish at our small café in Homer but it makes it onto the lodge menu from time to time. We use organic, short-grain brown rice that we make in a rice cooker.

2 SMALL RED POTATOES

1 TABLESPOON SALT

1 BUNCH SWISS CHARD

½ POUND DOMESTIC
MUSHROOMS

1 SMALL YELLOW ONION

1 TABLESPOON CANOLA OIL

SALT AND FRESHLY GROUND
BLACK PEPPER

¼ POUND BREAKFAST SAUSAGE
(SUCH AS CHICKEN APPLE OR
REINDEER), CUT INTO ½-INCH
SLICES

4 SPRIGS CHOPPED FRESH THYME

5 TEASPOONS LIGHT
SESAME OIL, DIVIDED

4 TEASPOONS UNSALTED
BUTTER

4 LARGE EGGS

4 CUPS COOKED SHORT-GRAIN
BROWN RICE

1 SMALL BUNCH CHIVES, MINCED

Wash the potatoes. Place them into a small pot with enough cold water to cover the potatoes by about 1 inch. Add in 1 tablespoon of salt. Bring the potatoes to a boil over high heat. Reduce the heat to medium-low and maintain the heat at a rapid simmer. Cook the potatoes until they are tender, about 8 minutes. Remove the potatoes and cool completely. Dice the potatoes into ¼-inch cubes.

Wash and destem the Swiss chard. Tear the leaves into bite-sized pieces. Dice the stems into ¼-inch pieces. Quarter the mushrooms. Peel, quarter, and slice the onion.

Heat the canola oil in a large sauté pan. Sauté the mushrooms and the onion over medium-high heat. Add in the potatoes and Swiss chard. Give the mixture a good toss and cook until all are cooked through and golden, about 7 minutes. Season with salt and pepper and set aside. Sear the sausage in a small nonstick sauté pan. Add the sausage to the vegetable mixture along with the thyme and 1 teaspoon of sesame oil. Toss the mixture.

In a small nonstick sauté pan, melt 1 teaspoon of butter over medium-low heat until the butter is frothy. Add in 1 teaspoon of the sesame oil. Crack in 1 egg and fry, flipping the egg over just after the whites set. Season to taste with salt and pepper. Repeat with the remaining 3 eggs (you might not need to add as much butter and oil with each egg).

Scoop 1 cup of the brown rice evenly into a wide 16-ounce Asian-style serving bowl. Ladle the sausage-vegetable mixture over the rice. Top the bowl with a fried egg and a sprinkle of chives.

Makes 4 servings.

CRISPY RUSSET POTATO AND GRUYÈRE HASH BROWNS

In Alaska, there are about a half-dozen varieties of starchy (Russet) potatoes that grow here. Alaska-grown Russet potatoes have interesting names like Hilat, Ranger, and Norkotah. We buy organic potatoes whenever possible.

3 SLICES THICK-SLICED BACON

1 POUND RUSSET POTATOES

1 LEEK, WHITE AND LIGHT GREEN PARTS ONLY, CUT IN HALF LENGTHWISE AND WASHED

SALT AND FRESHLY GROUND BLACK PEPPER

1 CUP GRATED GRUYÈRE CHEESE

In a medium ovenproof sauté pan, fry the bacon until crispy. Reserve 1 tablespoon of the bacon grease. Crumble the bacon and set aside.

Wash the outside of the potatoes and pat dry. Grate the potatoes on the largest hole of a box grater. To dry the potatoes, I like to put them into the center of a cotton dish towel and wring the towel to get out as much excess water as possible. If you have a potato ricer, this works well for squeezing the excess water out of the grated potatoes as well. The key to crispy hash browns is to get as much water out as possible. Slice the leeks and add them to the potatoes.

Heat the same sauté pan, adding back in the reserved bacon grease. When the pan is hot, spread the potatoes evenly in the pan. Season with salt and pepper. Cook the potatoes for about 5 minutes. Flip the potatoes over (you can slide the potatoes onto a plate and use this to invert them back into the pan) and sprinkle the cheese across the top of the potatoes. Cook for another 5 minutes. If you want the cheese to be browned and crispy, heat the pan under a broiler for 1 or 2 minutes. Sprinkle the crumbled bacon over the potatoes. Slide the potatoes out from the pan, portion, and serve.

Makes 4 to 6 servings.

MONKEY BREAD

This convenient breakfast bread allows guests to pluck off as much as they like from the loaf. Consider adding raisins or dried cherries into the cinnamon sugar mix.

3 TEASPOONS POWDERED
   CINNAMON, DIVIDED

1½ CUPS GRANULATED SUGAR,
   DIVIDED

6 TABLESPOONS ALL-PURPOSE
   FLOUR

2 TABLESPOONS UNSALTED
   BUTTER, SOFTENED

1 POUND BRIOCHE DOUGH
   (SEE PAGE 207)

Grease well a 9-by-5-inch loaf pan. Preheat the oven to 325°F.

Combine 2 teaspoons of the powdered cinnamon and 1 cup of the sugar to dip the monkey bread into. Set aside. Combine the remaining teaspoon of cinnamon, the remaining ½ cup sugar, the flour, and the butter to make a streusel topping. This should be the consistency of small peas.

Roll out the brioche dough to 1-inch thickness on a lightly floured surface. Cut the dough into ¾-inch pieces. It's OK if the pieces are misshapen. Toss the dough pieces into the cinnamon sugar mixture. Layer the pieces of brioche dough into the prepared loaf pan. The pieces don't need to be packed in too tightly. Sprinkle the streusel over the top of the bread. Place the loaf pan into the oven on the center rack. Bake for 30 minutes or until golden brown and cooked through the middle.

Makes 1 loaf monkey bread.

BRIOCHE DOUGHNUTS WITH CIDER BLACK CURRANT MARMALADE

Doughnuts can always be tricky to pull off early in the morning, but this recipe makes it easy by using brioche dough prepared the night before.

For the Brioche Doughnuts

1 CUP GRANULATED SUGAR

½ TEASPOON GROUND CARDAMOM

1 TEASPOON LEMON ZEST

1 POUND BRIOCHE DOUGH (SEE PAGE 207)

CANOLA OIL FOR FRYING

For the Cider Black Currant Marmalade

3 POUNDS (6 CUPS) BLACK CURRANTS

1 CUP APPLE CIDER

3 CUPS GRANULATED SUGAR

JUICE OF 1 LEMON

TO MAKE THE DOUGHNUTS: Mix together the sugar, cardamom, and lemon zest into a large mixing bowl. Set aside.

Roll the brioche dough out onto a lightly floured surface to 1-inch thickness. Using a 3-inch doughnut cutter, cut out 15 doughnuts.

Heat 2 to 3 inches of oil in a heavy, high-sided pot over medium heat until the oil reaches 350°F. Working in batches, drop the doughnuts into the oil and fry until they float. Turn the doughnuts over in the oil and continue cooking. Cook the doughnuts, turning them once or twice more as necessary, until they are uniformly browned, then transfer them to a plate lined with paper towel to drain.

While the doughnuts are still warm, dip them into the cardamom sugar mixture. Serve warm with our Cider Black Currant Marmalade.

Makes 15 doughnuts.

CIDER BLACK CURRANT MARMALADE

This is a natural old-style marmalade made without pectin. We serve it at the kitchen table along with our brioche doughnuts as well as other breakfast breads.

Clean the currants top and tail of any bits of stem or leaf. Wash them well in a colander and drain well.

Combine the currants, cider, sugar, and lemon juice in a large saucepan. Crush the black currants with the back of a spoon. Bring the mixture to a hard boil, reduce to a low simmer and cook until just beginning to gel, the skins are soft, and the mixture has thickened.

The timing on this can vary depending on the fruit, but it can take up to a couple hours to gel. To test if the marmalade is thick enough, place a tablespoon of the hot marmalade onto a chilled plate. Put the plate into the freezer until the marmalade is room temperature. Run your finger through the middle of the mixture. The two sides should combine together again.

Skim off any foam on top of the marmalade with a spoon. Place the marmalade into sterilized 8-ounce jars.

Makes about 5 (8-ounce) jars of marmalade.

BLUEBERRY PANCAKES WITH BERRY SYRUP

We have been using this recipe in our kitchen for several years with great success. Of course, we make much larger batches. You can substitute sourdough for the buttermilk if you have it on hand.

For the Blueberry Pancakes

2 CUPS ALL-PURPOSE FLOUR

2 TABLESPOONS GRANULATED SUGAR

2 TEASPOONS BAKING POWDER

1 TEASPOON BAKING SODA

2 LARGE EGGS, SEPARATED

1½ CUPS BUTTERMILK

½ TEASPOON PURE VANILLA EXTRACT

½ TEASPOON ORANGE ZEST

¼ TEASPOON SALT

4 TABLESPOONS UNSALTED BUTTER, MELTED

2 CUPS FRESH BLUEBERRIES

For the Berry Syrup

2 CUPS FRESH MIXED BERRIES

1 CUP PURE MAPLE SYRUP

TO MAKE THE PANCAKES: In a large mixing bowl, whisk together the flour, sugar, baking powder, and baking soda.

In a medium mixing bowl, whisk together the egg yolks, buttermilk, vanilla, orange zest, salt, and melted butter.

In the bowl of a stand mixer with the whisk attachment, whisk the egg whites to medium peaks.

Add the egg yolk-buttermilk mixture to the dry ingredients, mixing lightly. Using a nonstick spatula, gently fold in the egg whites until all is combined.

Preheat a griddle or skillet. Grease well. Ladle ¼ cup of the batter onto the griddle and sprinkle with about 2 tablespoons of blueberries. Cook the pancake until the edges are set and bubbles form on the surface, about 3 minutes. Using a wide spatula, flip the pancakes and cook for an additional 1 to 2 minutes or until the bottom is lightly browned. Repeat with the remaining batter.

TO MAKE THE SYRUP: In a small saucepan over medium heat, simmer the maple syrup and the fresh mixed berries together until they are combined.

FOR SERVING: Unsalted butter

TO SERVE: Pour the syrup over the pancakes and serve with a small pat of unsalted butter.

Makes 16 (3-inch) pancakes.

APPLE CHEDDAR WAFFLES

Waffles benefit from a gentle hand. Simply fold the ingredients together without over-stirring. In our recipe below, the eggs and buttermilk work best together if they are at room temperature. If you have the time, whip the egg whites and fold them in to create a lighter, fluffy version like our pancakes. Of course, there are many flavors that can be added to waffle batter and plenty of toppings to try, but we prefer Cheddar and sharp green apple with bacon slices added in. We top our waffles with simple sautéed apple compote.

2 CUPS ALL-PURPOSE FLOUR

1 TEASPOON BAKING SODA

1½ TEASPOONS BAKING POWDER

1 TEASPOON SALT

2 EGGS, WELL BEATEN

2 CUPS BUTTERMILK

2 TEASPOONS HONEY

3 TABLESPOONS UNSALTED BUTTER, MELTED

1 CUP SHREDDED SHARP CHEDDAR CHEESE

1 TART GREEN APPLE (SUCH AS GRANNY SMITH), CORED AND DICED

4 SLICES BACON, COOKED UNTIL CRISPY (OPTIONAL)

Combine the flour, baking soda, baking powder, and salt. Add in the eggs and buttermilk. To liquefy the honey a bit, add the honey to the butter as you melt it and combine both into the waffle batter. Fold in the cheese and apple bits (and bacon if desired).

Commercial waffle makers vary in style and instructions. Pour the recommended amount of batter into a prepared waffle iron (I usually lightly butter even a nonstick waffle iron) and cook for recommended length of time (usually no more than 5 minutes).

Makes 6 to 10 waffles, depending on your waffle maker.

CRAB CAKES BENEDICT WITH HOLLANDAISE SAUCE AND HONEY ENGLISH MUFFINS

This recipe collection includes recipes for our Crab Cakes, Honey English Muffins, Hollandaise Sauce, and how to perfectly poach an egg. We make this dish routinely but you may wish to make it a special Sunday morning ritual.

2 HONEY ENGLISH MUFFINS

4 CRAB CAKES

4 POACHED EGGS

HOLLANDAISE SAUCE

For the Honey English Muffins

1½ CUPS WHOLE MILK

3 TABLESPOONS UNSALTED
  BUTTER

1 TABLESPOON HONEY

2 TEASPOONS ACTIVE DRY YEAST

4 CUPS BREAD FLOUR

1 TEASPOON SALT

1 TEASPOON BAKING SODA

1 LARGE EGG, BEATEN

CORNMEAL FOR DUSTING
  THE BAKING SHEET

For the Crab Cakes

½ POUND SCALLOPS

1 POUND PICKED ALASKA
  LUMP CRABMEAT

1 SHALLOT, MINCED

1 TABLESPOON LEMON JUICE

1 CLOVE GARLIC, MINCED

1 TABLESPOON FINELY MINCED
  FLAT-LEAF PARSLEY

SALT AND FRESHLY GROUND
  BLACK PEPPER

HONEY ENGLISH MUFFINS

English muffins are surprisingly easy to make, even more quick and simple than bread. This particular recipe doesn't take a long time to rise. It is perfect for our Crab Cakes Benedict—or, to serve with a hot slab of butter and homemade jam.

TO MAKE THE ENGLISH MUFFINS: Preheat the oven to 350°F.

Place the milk and butter into a small saucepan over medium heat. Heat just until the butter is melted and the milk is warm. Cool slightly and then stir in the honey and yeast.

In the bowl of a stand mixer, combine the flour, salt, and baking soda. Add in the milk-butter-yeast mixture and the egg. Fitted with the paddle attachment, mix all until a dough forms.

Turn the dough out onto a well-floured surface. Roll the dough out with a flour-dusted rolling pin to about 1-inch thickness.

Use a round 3-inch cutter to cut out each muffin. Tradition calls for laying the muffins out onto a baking sheet sprinkled with cornmeal and we like this—the muffins don't get too floury and the cornmeal can be dusted off after baking if preferred. Sprinkle the top of the muffins with cornmeal also to prevent sticking.

Cover the muffins with a clean kitchen towel and let them rise for about 30 minutes.

Over a hot, lightly greased griddle, "griddle" each muffin for about 5 minutes on each side. Slip the muffins onto a baking sheet sprinkled with cornmeal and slide into the oven for an additional 8 to 10 minutes, or until the muffins are fully dried out in the center but still just lightly golden brown on the outside.

Makes 16 (3-inch) muffins.

For the Poached Eggs

4 LARGE EGGS

CANOLA OIL

For the Hollandaise Sauce

6 TABLESPOONS CLARIFIED
BUTTER (SEE PAGE 208)

3 EGG YOLKS

2 TEASPOONS LEMON JUICE

1 TEASPOON HOT PEPPER SAUCE
(OPTIONAL)

SALT AND FRESHLY GROUND
BLACK PEPPER

CRAB CAKES

Crab cake recipes are often full of bread and other fillers. We use some scallop meat (or alternately shrimp) to bind the crab together

TO MAKE THE CRAB CAKES: Purée the scallops in a food processor.

Drain the crabmeat and squeeze it dry (We use moistened cheesecloth for this). Coarsely dice the crabmeat if necessary.

Put the crab and scallops into a medium mixing bowl. Add in the shallot, lemon juice, garlic, and parsley. Mix well. Season the crab mixture with salt and pepper. The scallops should add enough textural glue to hold the crab cakes together but they will be delicate.

Form the crab into four 3-inch cakes. Place them onto a plastic wrap–lined baking sheet and chill in the refrigerator for about 30 minutes before cooking.

39

Preheat the oven to 350°F.

Gently remove the crab cakes from the baking sheet and set aside. Remove the plastic wrap from the baking sheet and grease the pan. Return the crab cakes to the baking sheet and place them into the oven on the center rack. Bake the crab for 3 to 5 minutes or until the cakes are just crisp on the edges and warmed through.

Makes 4 to 6 crab cakes.

POACHED EGGS

You are probably familiar with poaching eggs, but try this fun and useful method in little "packets" that will provide you with perfectly shaped eggs every time.

TO MAKE POACHED EGGS: Bring about 4 inches of water to a boil in a wide saucepan, then to a low simmer.

Take some plastic wrap and cut it into 4 pieces, each about double the size of the inside of a teacup. Oil the top side of each piece of the plastic wrap well. Take 4 teacups and line each with a piece of the plastic

wrap, oiled side up. Crack 1 egg into each of the teacups. Gather the plastic wrap up and twist tightly to remove any air from the egg "packets." Tie each packet with kitchen string.

Fill a medium mixing bowl with cold water. Set aside.

Drop each egg packet into the simmering water. Poach, trying to keep the packets submerged for about 5 minutes. Remove the packets from the water, cut off the tie with scissors, and remove the poached eggs. Drop them into the bowl of cold water to hold while assembling the Crab Cakes Benedict.

HOLLANDAISE SAUCE

We prefer a lemony-flavored hollandaise sauce for our crab cakes but you could add in herbs such as tarragon, or for a little classic luxury add in a bit of orange zest.

TO MAKE THE HOLLANDAISE SAUCE: Place the egg yolks, lemon juice, and hot sauce (if using) into a blender. Blend until the mixture is foamy and slightly stiffened.

With the blender running, gradually add the clarified butter in a thin stream.

Season to taste with the salt and pepper.

The sauce should be served within an hour. Keep in a warm spot.

Makes 1½ cups sauce.

TO ASSEMBLE THE CRAB CAKES BENEDICT: Toast the English muffins. Place one English muffin half onto a plate and top with one crab cake. Place a poached egg on top of the crab cake. Spoon over some of the hollandaise sauce.

Makes 4 servings.

HERBED BUTTERMILK BISCUITS WITH SMOKED SALMON

This is a pretty traditional biscuit recipe in which we've added in flaked hot-smoked salmon and Cheddar cheese. These biscuits are fantastic filled with dressed herbs and served with a creamy tomato soup, or slathered with butter or cream cheese at the breakfast table.

2 CUPS ALL-PURPOSE FLOUR

I TABLESPOON GRANULATED
  SUGAR

2 TEASPOONS BAKING POWDER

½ TEASPOON BAKING SODA

½ TEASPOON SALT

½ CUP (I STICK) UNSALTED
  BUTTER, CHILLED, CUT INTO
  SMALL PIECES

2 TABLESPOONS CHOPPED
  FRESH THYME

½ CUP GRATED SHARP
  CHEDDAR CHEESE

¼ CUP HOT-SMOKED (KIPPERED)
  SALMON

I CUP BUTTERMILK

Heat the oven to 400°F.

In a large mixing bowl, stir together the flour, sugar, baking powder, baking soda, and salt. Cut in the butter with a fork until the mixture looks like cornmeal. Add in the thyme, cheese, and smoked salmon. Gently toss to combine thoroughly.

Stir in the buttermilk until the dough leaves the sides of the bowl and is soft and sticky. You might use slightly less or more than the I cup called for depending on your flour.

On a lightly floured surface, lightly knead the dough. Roll the dough out to about 1-inch thickness. Cut the biscuits out with a 2-inch biscuit cutter. Place the biscuits about 1 inch apart onto an ungreased baking sheet.

Place the baking sheet in the center of the oven and bake for 15 minutes or until golden brown.

Makes 12 (2-inch) biscuits.

DANISH PASTRY USING QUICK DANISH DOUGH

Danish dough is a workhorse in our kitchen. We use it for many different recipes.

For the Quick Danish Dough

1 TABLESPOON ACTIVE DRY YEAST

½ CUP WHOLE MILK, WARM

¼ CUP GRANULATED SUGAR

ZEST OF 1 ORANGE

½ TEASPOON GROUND CARDAMOM

1 TEASPOON PURE VANILLA EXTRACT

2 LARGE EGGS, LIGHTLY WHISKED

¼ CUP FRESH ORANGE JUICE

3 CUPS ALL-PURPOSE FLOUR (PLUS EXTRA FOR DUSTING)

PINCH OF SALT

1½ CUPS (3 STICKS) UNSALTED BUTTER, CHILLED, SLICED

For the Filling

4 TART GREEN APPLES (SUCH AS GRANNY SMITH), PEELED, CORED, AND FINELY CHOPPED

½ CUP RAISINS

1 TEASPOON GROUND CINNAMON

¼ CUP LEMON JUICE

½ CUP LIGHT BROWN SUGAR

4 TABLESPOONS (½ STICK) UNSALTED BUTTER, MELTED

¼ CUP GRANULATED SUGAR

¼ CUP WHOLE MILK

TO MAKE THE DOUGH: Combine the yeast and milk into the bowl of a stand mixer fitted with the paddle attachment. Mix at low speed. Add in the sugar, orange zest, cardamom, vanilla extract, eggs, and orange juice.

Combine the flour and the salt in a separate small mixing bowl.

Change the mixer attachment on the stand mixer to the dough hook. Add in the flour mixture to the mixer bowl. Add in the butter, just pulsing the machine lightly several times so you don't warm the butter up. Turn the dough out onto a lightly floured surface and wrap in plastic wrap. It will be sticky. Chill the dough in the refrigerator for 1 to 2 hours.

Remove the dough from the plastic wrap. Sprinkle both the dough and a work surface lightly with flour. Roll the dough out to form a 9-by-12-inch rectangle. Press the dough down with a rolling pin to roll it out, covering any exposed bits of butter with a little flour. It will be quite soft.

Fold the dough into thirds, like a business letter, and press-roll it slightly. Roll out the folded dough back into a 9-by-12-inch rectangle. Repeat the process one more time (fold in thirds, roll into a 9-by-12-inch rectangle).

Fold the dough a final time into thirds. Wrap the folded dough in plastic wrap and refrigerate until ready to use, at least 2 hours.

TO MAKE THE FILLING: Preheat the oven to 350°F. Line a baking sheet with parchment.

Combine the apple, raisins, cinnamon, lemon juice, and brown sugar in a medium mixing bowl. Add the butter to a medium sauté pan and cook for about 6 to 8 minutes. Add in the apple mixture and sauté until the apples are softened, about 10 minutes. Remove the apple mixture and spread out onto the baking sheet to cool. Move the apple mixture to a medium mixing bowl when it is completely cooled.

TO MAKE THE DANISH PASTRY: Reline the baking sheet with parchment. Roll the dough into a 15-by-20-inch rectangle that is ¼ inch thick. Spread the apple mixture evenly over the dough, leaving a ½-inch edge

around the entire dough. You might not need all the apple mixture, depending on the size of your apples. Starting at the long end, roll the dough Swiss-roll style to form a log. Use a small, sharp knife to cut the log into 12 discs. Place each disc, cut-side down, on the lined tray, leaving room for spreading. Set aside in a warm draft-free place for 15 minutes to rise. Bake in the preheated oven for 15 minutes or until golden brown and cooked through. Remove from oven and set aside on the tray to cool.

Combine the sugar and the milk in a small mixing bowl to make a smooth paste. Place the icing into a resealable bag. Snip the end of the bag with scissors and drizzle the icing evenly over the Danish pastries.

Makes 12 Danish pastries.

RED-FLANNEL HASH

We serve this sometimes with corned beef and other times as a vegetarian option, usually with a poached egg. We like to bake the beets, which allows the outer skin to peel easily. For hash, we also prefer to bake or pan-roast vegetables rather than boil them.

2 MEDIUM RED BEETS

3 TABLESPOONS CANOLA OIL

1 MEDIUM SWEET POTATO, PEELED AND CUT INTO ½-INCH CUBES

4 MEDIUM RED POTATOES, CUT INTO ¼-INCH DICE

1 RED ONION, CHOPPED

1 CLOVE GARLIC, PEELED AND MINCED

SALT AND FRESHLY GROUND BLACK PEPPER

PINCH OF SMOKED PAPRIKA

1 SMALL BUNCH SWISS CHARD, CHOPPED

1 BAY LEAF

1 SPRIG THYME

1 TABLESPOON MINCED CHIVES

1 POUND CORNED BEEF, SHREDDED (OPTIONAL)

Preheat the oven to 350°F.

Wrap each beet in aluminum foil. Set them onto the middle rack of the oven. Bake the beets for 45 to 50 minutes, until they are soft.

In the meantime, heat the oil over medium-high heat in a heavy (we like to use cast iron) large skillet. Add in the sweet potato, red potatoes, onion, and garlic. Season the mixture with salt, pepper, and the paprika. Cook the vegetable mixture over medium heat for about 5 to 7 minutes. Cover the skillet with aluminum foil and place it into the oven next to the beets.

Continue to cook the beets and the vegetable skillet in the oven for about 30 to 35 minutes. Remove the skillet and set it aside, leaving it covered.

Continue to cook the beets for an additional 15 to 20 minutes or until they are soft and cooked through. Remove the beets from the oven and remove them from the aluminum foil.

After the beets have cooled slightly, about 5 to 6 minutes, rub off the skins using a kitchen towel or paper towel. Dice the beets and add them into the potato mixture. Add in the Swiss chard, bay leaf, and thyme.

Heat the skillet mixture over the stove for about 5 minutes to brown and crisp the potatoes. Sprinkle the chives over the hash. Add in the corned beef if desired. We serve red-flannel hash with poached eggs (see page 40) and toast.

Makes 6 servings.

SALMON BACON WITH RHUBARB LACQUER

We like serving these little crispy salmon pieces as a bacon alternative for breakfast. They can be broken into small shards for elegant additions to the appetizer tray as well.

6 OUNCES ALASKA COLD-SMOKED
SALMON LOX (ABOUT 10 SLICES)

½ POUND RHUBARB, WASHED,
TRIMMED, AND CHOPPED

½ CUP HONEY

½ CUP APPLE CIDER

½ SHALLOT, SLICED

1 TEASPOON FRESHLY GROUND
COARSE BLACK PEPPER

Preheat the oven to 350°F. Cover a baking sheet with aluminum foil. Coat the foil with spray release or with oil. Lay down each of the pieces of salmon onto the baking sheet. Set aside.

Place the rhubarb, honey, apple cider, shallot, and about a teaspoon of black pepper into a small heavy-bottomed saucepan. Heat over medium-low heat until the rhubarb is cooked and begins to fall apart. Add a little additional apple cider if more liquid is necessary. Cook for about 30 minutes until the mixture has reduced down to a thick syrupy consistency.

Brush the salmon with the rhubarb lacquer. Place the baking sheet onto the center rack of the oven and bake for about 5 to 6 minutes or until the bacon is just crisp.

Makes about 10 slices of bacon.

HUEVOS RANCHEROS

We break tradition by adding in Alaska smoked salmon.

¼ POUND MEXICAN SOFT-STYLE CHORIZO, CASINGS REMOVED

2 PACKAGES (4 OUNCES) MEXICAN DRIED CHILES, SPLIT AND SEEDED

2 CLOVES GARLIC, PEELED

2 TEASPOONS APPLE CIDER VINEGAR

SALT AND FRESHLY GROUND PEPPER

¾ TEASPOON GRANULATED SUGAR

¼ TEASPOON GROUND CUMIN

8 (4-INCH) FLOUR TORTILLAS

½ CUP SHREDDED SHARP CHEDDAR CHEESE

4 TEASPOONS UNSALTED BUTTER

4 LARGE EGGS

1 CUP COOKED AND HEATED PINTO BEANS

1 CUP SIMPLE SALSA (SEE PAGE 216)

½ POUND ALASKA HOT-SMOKED (KIPPERED) SALMON, SKINNED AND FLAKED

1 SMALL BUNCH CILANTRO

½ CUP SHREDDED MANCHEGO CHEESE

1 SMALL BUNCH GREEN ONION, GREEN PART MINCED

1 LIME, QUARTERED

Preheat the oven to 350°F. Line a 13-by-18-inch baking sheet with aluminum foil.

Crumble the chorizo into a medium sauté pan over medium heat. Cook thoroughly for about 5 minutes. Remove the chorizo and drain any grease from the pan, wiping it with a paper towel.

Heat the sauté pan over medium-low heat and toast the chiles two or three at a time, turning them while they are heating. They'll change color slightly in the process.

Soak the chiles in enough cold water to cover until they're soft, about 30 minutes. Drain the chilies and pat them dry.

Put a half cup of water into a blender with the soaked chiles along with the garlic, vinegar, one teaspoon salt, the sugar, and ground cumin. Blend until smooth, adding in a bit more water if necessary to purée. Add the chile mixture into the cooked chorizo.

Heat the tortillas in a large nonstick sauté pan over medium heat. Place them onto the baking sheet. Sprinkle the tortillas with the Cheddar cheese. Place the baking sheet into the oven to melt the cheese. Remove the pan from the oven and place each tortilla onto a warmed plate.

In a small nonstick sauté pan, melt one teaspoon of butter over medium-high heat and fry one egg until it is set, about one minute. Slide the egg onto one of the tortillas. Repeat with the remaining eggs.

Add some of the chorizo-chile sauce onto each tortilla. Spoon on some of the beans, some salsa, some flaked hot-smoked salmon, and a few sprigs of cilantro. Sprinkle each dish with some Manchego cheese and a little green onion. Season with salt and pepper. Serve immediately with a wedge of lime.

Makes 4 servings.

TUTKA BAY SUMMER GRANOLA

We make granola at least once a week and change it up for summer and winter. What isn't used for breakfast parfaits goes into trail mix or cookie batters. Add plenty of fresh fruit when serving.

6 CUPS ROLLED OATS

½ CUP STEEL-CUT OATS

2 CUPS NUTS AND SEEDS OF YOUR CHOICE

¼ CUP BLUEBERRY JUICE CONCENTRATE (OPTIONAL)

½ CUP CANOLA OIL

¼ CUP PACKED LIGHT BROWN SUGAR

½ CUP HONEY

1 TEASPOON SALT

1 CUP DRIED BLUEBERRIES

1 CUP DRIED CHERRIES

Preheat the oven to 300°F. Grease two 13-by-18-inch baking sheets.

Combine the rolled oats, the steel-cut oats, the nuts, seeds, and optional blueberry juice concentrate together, mixing them well with your hands.

Add in the oil, brown sugar, honey, and salt and mix.

Spread the granola onto the baking sheets. Bake for about 30 to 40 minutes, watching closely toward the end so the edges don't burn. We like to turn the granola once or twice while baking.

Remove from the oven and cool completely. Add in the dried blueberries and cherries. Store the granola in glass jars or sealable plastic bags to stay fresh.

SOME IDEAS FOR NUTS: slivered almonds, whole almonds, pecans, macadamia nuts, walnuts, or cashews.

SOME IDEAS FOR DRIED FRUITS: cranberries, blueberries, cherries, unsweetened coconut, figs, or apricots.

SOME IDEAS FOR SEEDS: flaxseed, sunflower seeds, and pumpkin seeds.

SOME IDEAS FOR SWEETENER: honey, maple syrup, rice syrup, birch syrup, or brown sugar.

SOME IDEAS FOR FLAVORING: lemon juice, blueberry juice concentrate, apple juice, cranberry juice concentrate, cinnamon, ground ginger, orange zest, ground cardamom, or nutmeg.

Makes 6 cups granola.

NO-KNEAD BREAKFAST BREAD

No-knead bread was introduced to me by my daughter Mandy who brings younger ideas into the kitchen, even though I am resistant to change. This style of bread gained popularity following the publication of cookbook author Jim Lahey's My Bread, from which this recipe is adapted.

3 CUPS BREAD FLOUR

1¼ TEASPOONS SALT

¼ TEASPOON ACTIVE DRY
   YEAST

1⅓ CUPS WATER
   (COOL, 55–65°F)

Combine the flour, salt, and yeast in a medium mixing bowl. Add in the water and stir to mix. Cover the bowl with a tea towel and set the bowl at room temperature for about 12 to 18 hours.

Remove the dough from the bowl. Shape it into a round by tucking in the edges of the dough into a bottom seam, cover the dough in a floured tea towel, and let rise again in a warm place for 2 hours. Preheat the oven to 475°F.

Put a heavy pot with a lid (like a cast-iron casserole or a Dutch oven) in the oven to heat. Carefully remove the hot pot from the oven and invert the dough into the pot, seam-side up.

Cover the pot and bake for 30 minutes. Remove the lid and continue to bake an additional 15 minutes or until the crust is a deep brown color. Cool the bread before slicing into it.

Makes 1 (10-inch) round.

HOT OAT CEREAL

We prefer steel-cut oats for breakfast. To make it easy, we cook the oats the night before so it is a quick process in the morning. If you don't want to bother with the overnight method, cook the oats for about 30 minutes. Often we add in a blend of equal parts of other grains such as triticale, barley flakes, whole-grain wheat, and bran.

4 CUPS WATER

1 CUP STEEL-CUT OATS

¼ TEASPOON SEA SALT

¼ CUP TOASTED WALNUTS

¼ CUP DRIED BLUEBERRIES

1 SWEET RED APPLE (SUCH AS RED DELICIOUS), WASHED AND SLICED

1 TABLESPOON ALMOND BUTTER

4 TABLESPOONS UNSALTED BUTTER

HONEY FOR THE TABLE

1 CUP WARMED ALMOND (OR OTHER) MILK

Bring the water to a boil in a heavy-duty medium saucepan with a lid. Add in the oats and salt. Stir the oats a few times, then turn off the heat. Leave the pot on the stove overnight.

In the morning, simply reheat the oats. Divide the oats into 4 serving bowls. Add in the walnuts, blueberries, apple, and almond butter. Serve with the butter, honey, and milk on the side.

Makes 4 servings.

WHOLE-GRAIN WILD BERRY BARS

These are a pleasant addition to our breakfast basket. We pack them along in the lunches we take on our out-camp expeditions.

1½ CUPS WHOLE-WHEAT FLOUR

1½ CUPS OLD-FASHIONED OATS

½ CUP PACKED LIGHT BROWN SUGAR

½ TEASPOON SALT

¾ CUP UNSALTED BUTTER, CHILLED, CHOPPED INTO ½-INCH CUBES

2 TABLESPOONS COLD WATER

1 CUP WILD BERRY JAM

Preheat the oven to 350°F. Grease a 9-by-13-inch baking dish, line it with parchment paper, and grease the parchment paper.

In the bowl of a food processor, combine the flour, oats, brown sugar, and salt. Pulse for 30 seconds. Add in the butter and cold water and pulse until the dough holds together when pressed.

Divide the dough mixture in half. Press one-half of the dough into the prepared baking dish, using a fork to press down evenly. Spread the preserves across the top of the dough.

Spread the remaining dough evenly on top of the preserves and gently press down.

Bake for 45 minutes, or until golden brown. Cool, cut into 3-by-3-inch bars, and serve. These bars are best kept at room temperature and will last 3 days.

Makes 12 bars.

WILD BERRY RICOTTA MUFFINS

These are beautiful and addictive muffins. Of course, you can use store-bought but this was a good excuse to include our simple recipe for homemade ricotta. And, if your berries aren't wild, the muffins will still be delicious.

2½ CUPS ALL-PURPOSE FLOUR, DIVIDED

¾ CUP LIGHT BROWN SUGAR, DIVIDED

1 TEASPOON GROUND ALLSPICE, DIVIDED

5 TABLESPOONS UNSALTED BUTTER, CHILLED, CUT INTO BITS

½ CUP GRANULATED SUGAR

1 TABLESPOON BAKING POWDER

¼ TEASPOON SALT

½ CUP (1 STICK) UNSALTED BUTTER, MELTED AND COOLED

2 LARGE EGGS

½ CUP WHOLE MILK

1 TEASPOON ORANGE ZEST

½ TEASPOON PURE VANILLA EXTRACT

½ CUP FRESH RICOTTA CHEESE (SEE PAGE 212)

1 CUP MIXED FRESH BERRIES

Preheat the oven to 375°F.

Grease a 12-cup muffin pan. Place the muffin pan onto a baking sheet.

To make the crumble, whisk together ½ cup of the flour, ½ cup brown sugar, and ½ teaspoon of the allspice into a small mixing bowl. Add in the cold butter and toss. Set aside.

To make the muffins, whisk together the remaining 2 cups of flour, the granulated sugar, baking powder, the remaining ½ teaspoon allspice, and salt into a large mixing bowl. Mix in the remaining ¼ cup of brown sugar.

In a separate medium mixing bowl, whisk together the melted butter, eggs, milk, orange zest, and vanilla extract until combined. Pour the liquid ingredients over the dry ingredients and whisk in to just mix. Gently fold in the ricotta and the berries.

Divide the batter evenly among the muffin cups. Sprinkle the crumble over each muffin, using your fingertips to gently press the crumble into the batter.

Place the baking sheet onto the middle rack of the oven. Bake for about 20 minutes, or until the tops are golden and a thin knife inserted into the center of the muffins comes out clean. Transfer the pan to a wire rack and cool for 5 minutes before carefully removing each muffin. Cool the muffins completely on the wire rack. Muffins can be stored, in an airtight container, at room temperature for up to 3 days.

Makes 12 muffins.

LET'S TAKE OUR LUNCHEON BY THE SEA

A PLEASANT WALK, A PLEASANT TALK ALONG THE BRINY BEACH . . .

Luncheon at the lodge is the most abbreviated meal of our day. Hummingbirds are buzzing through the garden, guests want to get back to their outdoor adventures, and employees are midstream into the rhythm of the workday. No lingering at the table for this meal. So, for guests, we offer a one-course luncheon served alongside a large platter of cookies or other portable sweets.

The type of meal service we offer at the lodge is called table d'hôte, literally translated as "table of the host," an ancient French culinary term used to describe meals that were included in lodging houses. For us, it means that our kitchen makes a menu selection for the day and offers that selection to our guests. Tutka Bay Lodge is small enough to find it difficult to source, prepare, and consume a large à la carte offering.

Each week, the kitchen team sits down together with fresh cups of coffee, sharpened pencils, and papers spread out onto the dining room table to craft the upcoming week's menu and shopping list. Influences might be the weather, the type of guests that will be visiting us, how many children are in the mix, or what is seasonally available. Mandy often makes a "road map" of the week on a large sheet of baking paper that she can hang on the door of the refrigerator. Every day of our summer season, we prepare breakfast, lunch, and dinner for guests as well as staff.

LET'S SERVE SOUP AT THE LODGE

Soup is served more often at lunch than any other meal. We might serve an elegant first-course soup at dinner, but it is a regular mainstay at the midday meal. When I was a young woman, I studied with French cookbook author Madeleine Kamman who once ran a restaurant in Cambridge. She impressed upon me how I should have a weekly rotating soup menu in my kitchen and the idea has captivated me ever since. Our soups change from year to year but they are always present in our culinary collection.

A FEW SIMPLE SOUP BASES AND STOCKS:

Tomato soup

Rough chop 4 or 5 large tomatoes and salt them well. Set aside for about 30 minutes. Purée the tomatoes in a food processor. Strain the tomatoes through a sieve, pressing the flesh. In a large saucepan, combine the tomato broth with equal part chicken stock or beef stock. Sauté 1 large yellow onion and 1 clove garlic, then add to the broth. Simmer until the flavors meld together. Serve with splashes of vinegar and olive oil, jumbo crouton, red onion, and fresh herbs. From there, you can add in rice, seafood, and other complements.

Mushroom Soup

Roast 2 pounds of mushrooms, 1 onion (quartered with skin on), and 2 garlic cloves for about 30 minutes in the oven at 350°F. Remove the skin from the onion, put the roasted mixture into a saucepan and cover with water. Simmer for about 30 minutes. Strain the stock through a sieve into a clean saucepan, pressing the flesh against the sieve. Discard the mushroom mixture. Heat the stock until reduced. This is the base for many soups in our kitchen, including Hungarian mushroom soup. Add in fresh sliced mushrooms, sour cream, lemon, parsley, and paprika.

One-Hour Chicken Stock

Roast 2 pounds of cut-up chicken wings in the oven. Brown 1 pound ground chicken thigh meat in the base of a pressure cooker. Add in the roasted chicken wings, 1 yellow onion, 2 small carrots, 1 leek, ½ cup flat-leaf parsley, and about 6 black peppercorns to the pressure cooker. Cover with water. Cook under pressure on 15 psi for about 1 hour. Strain.

Quick Beef Stock

Roast 2 pounds of beef shank in the oven. Brown 1 pound of ground beef in the base of a pressure cooker. Add in the beef shank, 1 yellow onion, 1 leek, 1 clove garlic, 2 small carrots, ½ cup flat-leaf parsley, a little red wine, and 6 black peppercorns to the pressure cooker. Cover with water. Cook under pressure on 15 psi for about 1 hour. Strain.

Homemade Clam Broth

Combine 1 large handful of cleaned and scrubbed clams, chopped clove of garlic, ½ cup flat-leaf parsley, 3 sprigs thyme, 1 cup dry white wine, and enough water to cover and simmer over medium heat for about 20 minutes. Strain the broth through a sieve. Pick out the remaining clam meat and use for another purpose. Clam broth can be used to make any seafood-based soup.

Quick Seafood Stock

Heat 1 tablespoon grapeseed oil in a large stockpot. Add in 1 pound of shrimp shells, 1 pound halibut bones, and 1 pound of crab shells and cook until the shells are bright red and a little bit smoky. Add in 1 cup dry white wine and scrape up any little bits of fish that might be on the bottom of the pan. Add in 1 yellow onion, 1 small leek, 1 carrot, 1 clove garlic, and 1 teaspoon fennel seeds. Pour in enough water to cover the shells. Bring to a boil, then reduce, and simmer about 20 minutes. Strain through a fine mesh strainer.

Sea Broth

Add 1 (5-inch) piece of dried kelp (kombu) to 5 cups of water and bring just to a boil. Turn off the heat and save the kombu. Add in 1 cup of dried bonito flakes. Let sit for a couple of minutes, and then pour through moistened cheesecloth. This is a broth taught to me by my beloved mentor Elizabeth Andoh.

THERE SHOULD ALWAYS BE SALAD ON THE TABLE

Salads are featured often on the luncheon menu. We are lucky to have a garden that gives us fresh greens throughout the summer, and we have access to a remarkable farmer's market and local farmer's network for plenty of fresh produce. If you are visiting Homer on Wednesdays or Saturdays, make sure to take time to stop by the market. Highlights often include local honey (some of the world's best), handmade jams and jellies, fresh seafood, oysters, soaps, flowers, jewelry, and more.

In Alaska, most quick-growing greens and herbs do well with our long summer days. At Tutka Bay

Lodge, we've had success with starting the season with cold-weather greens like Black Seeded Simpson, Arctic King, and Astro. As the weather and soils warm up, we add in new greens that will last to the end of the summer, like red butter-worth and Tyee. We like to make fresh green salads that are hefty mixtures of herbs, greens, and something crunchy like nuts or croutons, something soft like cheese or dried fruits, something crispy like slices of Granny Smith apple, and maybe something chewy like beans and grains.

TO DRESS A SALAD: Make sure the greens are soaked in cold water and perfectly dry. Place most of the dressing into the bottom of your salad bowl. Add in the greens and toss. Pour the remaining dressing over the top. Plate the greens, usually about 1 handful, or 1 cup, of greens per serving, into the center of a plate. Sprinkle on garnishes like fresh berries, cheese, red onion, fresh edible flowers, or nuts.

We certainly look to local wild edibles that we can add to our salad bowl. At Tutka Bay Lodge, we find beach peas down by the water's edge. There's some controversy about beach peas. Some people in Alaska consider them nonedible but we find them beautiful and delicious.

* *SEA LETTUCE makes an abundant presence along our shoreline. It's identifiable by its vivid green color. I always ask tide-pooling guests to bring back a little sea lettuce to the kitchen. We overwhelmingly prefer to simply wash the lettuce lightly and dry it in the sun to crumble onto salads.*

* *I have been blessed with wild fields of RED CURRANTS everywhere I have lived in Alaska. For over thirty years, I've never been through a summer without gathering currants. We toss them into dishes with abandon, and make sauces, jellies, and savory concoctions with them.*

* *I've only seen a couple of bears in the few years we have lived at the lodge, but they were all after the thick blankets of BLUEBERRIES that cover our property. We use the berries both fresh and preserved, and the leaves in tea and aromatics. Sometimes we gather leaves and throw them onto the barbecue for aromatic smoke.*

* *ROSES in Alaska produce giant hips in the fall and we harvest them as soon as it frosts. They are delicious in tea—simply chop up some hips, pour boiling water over them, and strain. Rose petal jam is a taste of summer most enjoyed in the depths of our winter. And rose petal butter is lovely over salmon.*

* *SALMONBERRY bushes are splashed all over our property. They have a lovely magenta-coral color that makes for a beautiful jelly and garnish to salads, but I love them the most for attracting the outrageous hummingbirds that live with us much of the summer. Sometimes the hummingbirds are so abundant, we can stand outside, with our arms stretched out, and be showered and swarmed by these tiniest of jeweled miracles.*

* *RASPBERRIES grow well at Tutka Bay Lodge and we have both wild and cultivated varieties found throughout the property. We sprinkle raspberries into salad with red onion and blue cheese. Or, we plunk them into a glass of champagne. Combine puréed raspberries with balsamic vinegar, a little butter, and a spoon of honey as a condiment for sandwiches and cheese appetizers.*

CURRIED FISH AND CHIPS

We love this British-style treatment of fish. We actually prefer cod rather than halibut but both are fantastic. We serve our fish and chips with mushy peas and crunchy potatoes, just like a London pub might.

2 POUNDS POTATOES

CANOLA OIL FOR FRYING

SALT

1 CUP ALL-PURPOSE FLOUR

1 TEASPOON HOMEMADE CURRY POWDER (SEE PAGE 213)

1 CUP BEER

2 LARGE EGG WHITES, WHIPPED TO SOFT PEAKS

1 POUND ALASKA COD OR HALIBUT FILLETS, BONELESS AND SKINLESS

Scrub the potatoes and cut them into thick wedges. Wash the potatoes well to remove extra starch from them. Pat the potatoes completely dry in a kitchen towel or paper towel.

Pour the canola oil into a deep casserole pan or an electric deep fat fryer. Heat the oil to 325°F. Blanch the cut potatoes in the oil until the potatoes are soft, but not colored, about 4 minutes. Remove and pat the potatoes dry. Heat the oil to 350°F and refry the potatoes until they are golden brown, another few minutes. Salt and set aside in a warm oven.

Mix together the flour, curry powder, and the beer, and then fold in the egg whites. Dip the fish in the batter. Using a fish spatula, lower the fish slowly into the oil (if you drop it in, the fish might sink and the batter will stick to the pan). The fish should fry for about 4 minutes or until the crust is a deep golden brown. Drain the fish on plenty of paper towels.

Makes 4 servings.

CHILLI-CRAB FRESH ROLLS WITH DIPPING SAUCE

We've been to Singapore several times and we love the hawker food markets. Chilli crab is a Singaporean sweet and garlicky spicy crab stew of sorts, messy and delicious. We've bypassed the main course approach and created an appetizer in honor of this national dish. We make our own Chile-Garlic Paste (see page 66) but you can purchase this in most Asian markets.

½ POUND ALASKA LUMP CRABMEAT

I TABLESPOON HONEY

JUICE OF ½ LEMON

I SMALL BUNCH GREEN ONIONS, DICED

4 TABLESPOONS CHILE-GARLIC PASTE (SEE PAGE 66)

4 OUNCES ASIAN RICE VERMICELLI (RICE STICKS)

TOASTED SESAME OIL

I PACKAGE ROUND VIETNAMESE RICE PAPER WRAPPERS

I CUP FRESH MINT LEAVES

I CUP FRESH BASIL

I CUP FRESH CILANTRO LEAVES

I CUCUMBER, PEELED AND CUT INTO ¼-INCH STICKS

I SMALL HEAD GREEN-LEAF LETTUCE, CLEANED AND SEPARATED INTO LEAVES

TO MAKE THE FRESH ROLLS: Mix the crab, honey, lemon juice, green onion, and chile-garlic paste together in a medium mixing bowl. Set aside.

Bring a medium saucepan filled two-thirds with water to a boil. Drop in the rice vermicelli and cook for about 2 to 3 minutes. Remove the noodles and shock them in cool water. Strain the noodles, removing any excess water. Place them into a medium mixing bowl and toss the noodles with a dash of sesame oil. Set aside.

Place the rice paper wrappers, marinated crabmeat, cooked and seasoned rice noodles, the mint, basil, cilantro, cucumber, and lettuce into wide medium bowls and arrange them onto your countertop in that order.

Place a clean, damp kitchen towel on a work surface. Fill a large mixing bowl with hot water. Working with one rice paper wrapper, completely submerge the wrapper until it is soft and pliable, about 15 seconds. Remove the wrapper from the water and place it onto the towel.

Working quickly, lay some of the crabmeat in a row just above the center of the wrapper. Layer some of the rice noodles over the crab, then some mint leaves, basil leaves, and some cilantro. Place some of the cucumber sticks on either side of the noodle pile. Fold some of the lettuce in half and then roll it into a cigar shape so you create a substantial layer of lettuce. Add this to the noodles pile.

Fold the bottom half of the rice paper wrapper over the filling. Holding the whole thing firmly in place, fold the sides of the wrapper in.

Then, pressing firmly down onto the roll to hold the folds in place, roll it up tightly from the bottom to the top.

For the Dipping Sauce

1 TABLESPOON ASIAN FISH
 SAUCE (NAM PLA)

JUICE OF 1 LIME

1 TABLESPOON SOY SAUCE

1 TABLESPOON HONEY

1 TABLESPOON CHILE-GARLIC
 PASTE (SEE BELOW)

1 CLOVE GARLIC, MASHED

1 TEASPOON TOASTED
 SESAME OIL

¼ CUP WATER

Turn the roll so that the seam faces downward and the row of crab faces upward. Place the completed fresh roll onto a rimmed baking sheet lined with plastic wrap. Cover the roll loosely with plastic wrap. Repeat with the remaining wrappers and fillings. Leave ¾ inch between each fresh roll on the sheet so they don't stick together, and replace the water in the pan or dish with hot water as needed. Cut the rolls in half if you have used large wrappers, and serve with the dipping sauce.

Makes 8 to 16 fresh rolls, depending on the size of wrapper you use.

TO MAKE THE SAUCE: Whisk fish the sauce, lime juice, soy sauce, honey, chile-garlic paste, garlic, sesame oil, and water together in a medium mixing bowl; set aside.

Makes ⅔ cup dipping sauce.

CHILE-GARLIC PASTE

This paste can be varied by using different chiles or combinations of chiles. Sometimes we add in honey depending on how we are using the paste. Be cautious when working with chiles. You may wish to wear plastic gloves and remember to avoid touching your eyes.

10 TO 15 WHOLE DRIED RED CHILES

2 TABLESPOONS CANOLA OIL

1 TEASPOON SALT

3 CLOVES GARLIC, PEELED AND
 MINCED

2 TABLESPOONS APPLE CIDER
 VINEGAR

Split the chiles in half and remove any seeds and stem. Put the chiles into a small mixing bowl and cover them with boiling water. Soak the chiles for about 30 minutes.

Put the chiles, oil, salt, and garlic in a food processor. Purée the chile mixture until smooth, adding in the vinegar.

Makes about ½ cup paste.

RUSSIAN SUMMER SOUP

We have plenty of cabbage in the garden and in the markets toward the end of the summer. This is a nice savory soup. It can accommodate many different types of vegetables. You can substitute vegetable stock and leave out the beef for a vegetarian option.

1 TABLESPOON CANOLA OIL

1 YELLOW ONION, PEELED, QUAR-
TERED, AND DICED

2 CLOVES GARLIC, MINCED

1 POUND LEAN GROUND BEEF

1½ TEASPOONS CARAWAY SEEDS

1 TEASPOON FRESH THYME

2 CARROTS, PEELED AND DICED

½ CUP MIXED WILD MUSHROOMS,
TORN INTO BITE-SIZED PIECES

1 MEDIUM TART GREEN APPLE
(SUCH AS GRANNY SMITH), PEELED
AND DICED

6 CUPS STORE-BOUGHT OR QUICK
BEEF STOCK (SEE PAGE 60)

2 LARGE TOMATOES, PEELED,
SEEDED, AND DICED

1½ TABLESPOONS HONEY

1 TEASPOON PAPRIKA

3 CUPS COARSELY CHOPPED
GREEN CABBAGE

1 TABLESPOON CIDER VINEGAR

SALT AND FRESHLY GROUND
BLACK PEPPER

Heat the oil in a large Dutch oven or heavy-bottomed stockpot over medium heat. Add in the onion and sauté over low heat until the onion is translucent, about 10 minutes. Add in the garlic, beef, caraway seeds, and thyme, stirring to break up the beef with a wooden spoon. Cook until the beef is mostly browned, an additional 5 minutes. Add in the carrots, mushrooms, and apple. Cook, stirring, for 2 to 3 minutes.

Stir in the broth, tomatoes, honey, and paprika. Adjust the heat to low and simmer gently for 10 minutes. Stir in the cabbage and cook until barely tender, 3 to 4 minutes more. Add in the vinegar and season to taste with the salt and pepper.

Makes 6 servings.

FISH TACOS WITH MANCHEGO-CORN TORTILLAS

We used halibut in the photo for this recipe but we often select cod, rockfish, or even salmon for this popular luncheon item.

For the Manchego-Corn Tortillas

1 TEASPOON SALT

1 TEASPOON GROUND CUMIN

2 CUPS MASA HARINA CORN FLOUR

2 CUPS HOT WATER

½ POUND GRATED MANCHEGO
    CHEESE

For the Fish Tacos

8 SMALL MANCHEGO-CORN
    TORTILLAS

JUICE OF 2 LIMES, DIVIDED

ZEST OF 2 LIMES, DIVIDED

¼ TEASPOON CUMIN

2 CLOVES GARLIC, PEELED
    AND MINCED

1 TEASPOON SALT

FRESHLY GROUND BLACK
    PEPPER

1 POUND HALIBUT, BONELESS
    AND SKINLESS

2 TABLESPOONS CANOLA OIL

⅓ CUP FRESH HONEY YOGURT
    (SEE PAGE 211)

⅓ CUP MEXICAN-STYLE WHITE CHEESE

1 SMALL RED CABBAGE, FINELY
    SHREDDED

1 AVOCADO, PEELED AND ROUGH
    CHOPPED

1 CUP SIMPLE SALSA (SEE PAGE 216)

2 TABLESPOONS PICKLED RED ONIONS
    (SEE PAGE 215)

1 SMALL LIME, CUT INTO SIXTHS

MANCHEGO-CORN TORTILLAS

We prepare corn tortillas as often as we prepare tortillas made from flour. We include cumin in this recipe as well as a little grated cheese.

TO MAKE THE TORTILLAS: Preheat a griddle or cast-iron skillet.

Mix the salt and the cumin into the masa harina corn flour. Slowly pour the hot water into the flour, adding in just enough to make a firm, but not dry or cracked, dough. Let the dough rest for about an hour, covered at room temperature.

Divide the dough and roll into 2-inch balls. Make an indentation in the center of each ball and place some of the cheese into the center. Reroll the dough into balls, covering the cheese with dough.

Roll or flatten the dough in a tortilla press into an ⅛-inch-thick disk. If you don't have a press, use a rolling pin. Place the disk onto a hot dry griddle or cast-iron skillet and cook until the top of the tortilla starts to brown, about 1 minute. Flip the disk over and heat for another minute or so.

Makes 12 (6-inch) tortillas.

TO MAKE THE TACOS: Preheat the oven to 425°F.

Stack the tortillas on top of each other and wrap them in aluminum foil. Place the tortillas into the oven to warm.

In a shallow medium mixing bowl, combine the juice of 1 lime, the zest of 1 lime, cumin, garlic, salt, and pepper to taste.

Cut the halibut into 1-inch pieces. Pat the halibut dry with a paper towel. Place the pieces in the lime-cumin mixture and let them sit for about 5 minutes.

Heat the canola oil in a medium sauté pan over medium heat. Add in the halibut and cook until just done.

Meanwhile, in a small mixing bowl, combine the yogurt, cheese, juice of 1 lime, and zest of 1 lime. Add in the shredded red cabbage and set aside.

Season the avocado chunks with salt and pepper and set aside.

To assemble the tacos, carefully open the foil packet of tortillas and allow the steam to escape. Lay the tortillas in a single layer on a cutting board. Spoon some salsa onto the center of each. Top each with a couple pieces of halibut, yogurt-cheese-cabbage mixture, avocado, and pickled red onion. Garnish with lime wedges.

Makes 4 servings.

RHUBARB LEMONADE BARS

These little bar cookies are summery and light and a perfect use for our abundant rhubarb in the garden. We've had some of our rhubarb plants for more than twenty years.

For the Crust

½ CUP (1 STICK) UNSALTED BUTTER, SOFTENED

¼ CUP GRANULATED SUGAR

½ TEASPOON SALT

2 TEASPOONS PURE VANILLA EXTRACT

2½ CUPS ALL-PURPOSE FLOUR

2 LARGE EGGS

For the Strawberry-Rhubarb Syrup

1 CUP FRESH STRAWBERRIES, SLICED

4 STALKS RHUBARB, DICED

PINCH SALT

1 CUP GRANULATED SUGAR, DIVIDED

3 TABLESPOONS CORNSTARCH

For the Filling

½ CUP (1 STICK) UNSALTED BUTTER

1¼ CUPS GRANULATED SUGAR

2 TABLESPOONS CORNMEAL

2 TABLESPOONS CORNSTARCH

PINCH SALT

4 LARGE EGGS

JUICE OF 3 LEMONS (ABOUT ½ CUP)

TO MAKE THE CRUST: Preheat the oven to 350°F. Lightly grease a 9-by-13-inch baking pan.

In a medium mixing bowl, cream the butter until fluffy. Add in the sugar, salt, and the vanilla extract. Stir in the flour and eggs, mixing until a soft dough is formed.

Press the dough into the bottom and up the sides of the prepared pan. Prick the dough all over with a fork. Bake the crust for 8 minutes. Set aside.

TO MAKE THE SYRUP: Combine the strawberries, rhubarb, salt, and ½ cup sugar in a small saucepan. Over low heat, stirring constantly, bring the mixture to a boil. Combine the cornstarch into ¼ cup of water in a small glass. Add the cornstarch dissolved in the water and the remaining sugar to the strawberry-rhubarb mixture. Return the mixture to a boil, remove it from the heat, and let the mixture cool slightly. Set aside.

TO MAKE THE FILLING: Melt the butter in a small saucepan. Add in the sugar, cornmeal, cornstarch, salt, eggs, and the lemon juice. Spread the mixture over the crust. Swirl in the strawberry-rhubarb syrup. Return the pan to the oven and bake for an additional 25 minutes, until the top is lightly browned and the edges are golden. Cool and cut into 36 bars (6 rows by 6 rows).

Makes 36 (2-inch-by-1½-inch) bars.

GINGER LIME SHRIMP STIR-FRY

This is an Alaska fast food recipe. We have a wok in my kitchen that we use for many quick-cook dishes. It is an elegant modern nonstick version with a clear lid. We serve this stir-fry over freshly mounded and steaming jasmine rice.

3 TABLESPOONS CANOLA OIL

1 POUND SPOT SHRIMP, PEELED, TAILS ON

1 TABLESPOON RICE WINE VINEGAR

JUICE OF 1 LIME

½ THAI BIRD CHILE, CHOPPED FINELY

1-INCH KNOB FRESH GINGER, PEELED AND SLICED THIN

2 CLOVES GARLIC, PEELED AND SLICED THIN

2 TABLESPOONS SOY SAUCE

¼ CUP SHREDDED THAI BASIL

Heat a wok or nonstick skillet over high heat. Pour in the canola oil and allow it to get very hot. Add in the shrimp, vinegar, lime juice, and chile. Allow the shrimp to cook about halfway 1 to 2 minutes. Add in the ginger, garlic, and soy sauce. Cook the shrimp through. Add in the basil.

Makes 1 pound stir-fry.

COD FRITTERS WITH PEA CREAM

We lovingly call these "cod balls" in our kitchen. This recipe has Spanish bone structure but we never use the more traditional salt cod in Alaska—why would we ever need to as we have plenty of fresh cod available. We serve these with a summer fresh pea cream

For the Cod Fritters

4 SMALL RED POTATOES

2 TABLESPOONS PURE OLIVE OIL

1 CLOVE GARLIC, MINCED

1 BUNCH GREEN ONIONS, MINCED

½ YELLOW ONION, PEELED, HALVED, AND MINCED

1 CUP WHOLE MILK

1 POUND BONELESS, SKIN-LESS COD

SALT AND FRESHLY GROUND BLACK PEPPER

½ TEASPOON NUTMEG

1 LEMON, CUT IN HALF

1 HANDFUL FLAT-LEAF PARSLEY, MINCED

2 LARGE EGGS

1 CUP ALL-PURPOSE FLOUR

1 CUP PANKO

OIL FOR DEEP FRYER

COARSE SEA SALT

TO MAKE THE FRITTERS: Wash the potatoes and quarter them. Drop them into salted boiling water. Cook the potatoes until they are tender, about 10 minutes. Drain and place the potatoes into a medium mixing bowl.

Heat 2 tablespoons of olive oil in a sauté pan. Add in the garlic, green onions, and yellow onion. Sauté over low heat until the onion is soft and translucent, about 10 minutes. Add in the milk. Bring the mixture to a simmer.

Cut the fish up into pieces that fit easily into your pan. Add the fish into the milk mixture. Poach the fish for about 5 to 7 minutes.

Lift the fish out of the milk mixture and add it into the bowl with the potatoes. Season the potatoes and fish with salt and pepper to taste. Add in the nutmeg, the juice of half a lemon, and the parsley. Mix the mixture lightly. You can vary the texture of the batter here either by blending well or leaving it a little chunky. Add in 1 egg and mix well. Refrigerate the fish mixture for about 30 minutes.

In the meantime, bring the deep fryer up to the temperature of 360°F. Crack the other egg into a small mixing bowl and mix with a fork. Put the flour and panko separately into two additional small bowls.

Shape about 1 ounce of the fish batter into a round ball. Dip the ball into the flour, then the egg, and finally the panko. Repeat with as many balls as you want to make. (Any leftover sautéed batter is great in eggs in the morning or in pasta for lunch.)

Lower one fish ball into the fryer to check the temperature. It will take about 2 to 3 minutes to cook, turning a light golden brown. Repeat.

Cut the remaining lemon half into wedges. Sprinkle the cod fritters with chunky sea salt if you prefer and serve with Pea Cream.

Makes 24 fritters.

For the Pea Cream

2 CUPS FRESH GARDEN PEAS, SHELLED

2 CUPS STORE-BOUGHT OR HOME-MADE ONE-HOUR CHICKEN STOCK (SEE PAGE 60)

1 LARGE SHALLOT

2 TABLESPOONS UNSALTED BUTTER

1 SPRIG THYME

COARSE SEA SALT

FRESHLY GROUND BLACK PEPPER

2 OUNCES DRY VERMOUTH

½ CUP HEAVY CREAM

PEA CREAM

Pea cream is a beautiful summer treasure that can be used for many different kinds of recipes, including as a stand-in for a nice pasta sauce thinned out a bit with chicken stock.

TO MAKE THE PEA CREAM: Wash the peas and drain them in a colander.

Bring the chicken stock to a boil, and then reduce the heat to a simmer.

Peel and slice the shallot finely. Heat a medium saucepan with the butter and sauté the shallot until tender with no color. Add in the peas, thyme, salt and pepper to taste, and cook for a couple of minutes.

Add the vermouth to the pan and stir, scraping up any bits of butter and shallot that may have adhered to the bottom of the pan. Add in the hot stock and the cream, stirring and maintaining a low simmer. Cook for a few minutes, until the peas are tender.

Pour the pea mixture into a blender and purée. Pour the pea blend through a fine mesh strainer into a medium serving bowl and serve with the cod fritters.

Makes 3 cups pea cream.

KACHEMAK BAY SEAFOOD CHOWDER

This is a luxurious and indulgent soup that we can "dress" up or down, and serve in different iterations all year long.

1 CUP DICED BACON

2 MEDIUM YELLOW ONIONS, PEELED, QUARTERED, AND SLICED

3 CARROTS, PEELED AND DICED

7 SMALL RED POTATOES, WASHED AND DICED

1 CLOVE GARLIC, MINCED

1 SPRIG THYME

SALT AND FRESHLY GROUND BLACK PEPPER

½ CUP DRY WHITE WINE

3 CUPS STORE-BOUGHT OR HOME-MADE ONE-HOUR CHICKEN STOCK (SEE PAGE 60)

3 CUPS HEAVY WHIPPING CREAM

1 POUND RED SALMON, CUT INTO 1-INCH CHUNKS

1 POUND COD, CUT INTO 1-INCH CHUNKS

1 POUND KODIAK BAY SCALLOPS

1 POUND SPOT SHRIMP, PEELED

6 OUNCES ALASKA LUMP CRABMEAT

1 SMALL BUNCH FLAT-LEAF PARSLEY, STEMMED AND CHOPPED

Place the bacon in a large heavy-bottomed saucepot, and cook over medium high heat to render out the fat. Remove and reserve the bacon from the pan but leave in the fat. Reduce the heat and add in the onions, carrots, and potatoes. Add in the garlic and thyme. Season with salt and pepper to taste.

Sauté the mixture until all is slightly tender, about 7 minutes. Add in the white wine and let the alcohol cook off for about a minute. Add in the stock and the cream.

Simmer the stock and vegetable mixture until the vegetables are cooked and the liquid has reduced slightly. Turn the heat to low. Stir in the salmon, cod, scallops, shrimp, and the crab. The seafood will poach in the hot liquid and will be done in a couple of minutes. Add in the reserved bacon. Season with additional salt and pepper if needed.

Spoon the chowder into 6 soup bowls. Sprinkle a little parsley onto the top before serving.

Makes 6 servings.

DUNGENESS CRAB MELTS

These sandwiches are delicious with a fresh garden salad or a cup of tomato soup. They are our most popular luncheon item.

1 LEEK, WHITE AND LIGHT GREEN PARTS ONLY, CUT IN HALF LENGTHWISE AND WASHED

½ CUP (1 STICK) UNSALTED BUTTER, DIVIDED

½ YELLOW ONION, PEELED, HALVED, AND SLICED

1 SPRIG THYME

1 CLOVE GARLIC, MINCED

2 CUPS DUNGENESS LUMP CRAB-MEAT

2 GREEN ONIONS, MINCED

4 TABLESPOONS AIOLI (SEE PAGE 207)

SALT AND FRESHLY GROUND BLACK PEPPER

4 SLICES SOURDOUGH BREAD, THICKLY SLICED

2 CUPS SHREDDED SHARP CHEDDAR CHEESE

2 TEASPOONS MINCED CHIVES

Preheat the oven to 350°F.

Combine the leek and ¼ cup of the butter in a small saucepan and place over low heat. Lightly poach the leeks for about 8 to 10 minutes. While the leeks are poaching, heat 1 tablespoon of butter in a small sauté pan. Add in the yellow onion, thyme, and garlic. Sauté the onion mixture over low heat until the onion is soft and caramelized. Set aside the leeks and onion.

Drain the crabmeat of any excess liquid. We often do this by wringing out the crab using moistened cheesecloth. In a medium mixing bowl, place the drained crab and pick through to remove any bones or carti-lage. Stir in the yellow onion mixture, leeks, green onions, and just enough aioli to hold it all together. Season with salt and pepper to taste.

Heat a medium sauté pan to medium heat and melt the remaining 3 tablespoons of butter. Toast 4 slices of bread in the butter until golden brown. Turn off the heat, leaving the bread in the sauté pan. Place some of the cheese on top of each slice of the bread. Spoon some of the crab-meat onto the 4 slices of bread. Place the melts into the oven until cheese is just melted and crab is warmed through, about 2 to 3 minutes. Sprinkle with the minced chives.

Makes 4 open-face sandwiches.

BLUEBERRY CREAM CHEESE COOKIES

We love the combination of cream cheese, chocolate, and blueberries. We recommend purchasing commercial "half-sheet pans," which are a slightly different size and thickness than home-style baking sheets.

4 CUPS ALL-PURPOSE FLOUR

2 TEASPOONS BAKING SODA

1 TEASPOON SALT (PLUS ADDITIONAL FOR SPRINKLING)

1½ CUPS UNSALTED BUTTER

2 TEASPOONS LEMON ZEST

1¼ CUPS LIGHT BROWN SUGAR

1¼ CUPS GRANULATED SUGAR

2 LARGE EGGS

2 TEASPOONS PURE VANILLA EXTRACT

2 CUPS SEMISWEET CHOCOLATE CHIPS

1 CUP FRESH BLUEBERRIES

4 TABLESPOONS CREAM CHEESE, COLD, CUT INTO SMALL PIECES

Preheat the oven to 325°F. Grease two 13-by-18-inch baking sheets or line with parchment paper. Set aside.

Sift the flour, baking soda, and salt into a medium mixing bowl. Set aside.

Cream the butter, lemon zest, brown sugar, and granulated sugar together until the mixture is light and fluffy either by hand or using a stand mixer. Add in the eggs, one at a time, mixing well after each addition. Stir in the vanilla.

Add in the dry ingredients and mix until just combined. Fold in the chocolate chips. Gently fold in the blueberries and cream cheese, trying not to break up the berries. Wrap the dough in plastic wrap and refrigerate until chilled, at least 30 minutes.

Divide the dough into 32 pieces, each piece about 3 tablespoons. Place the dough onto the baking sheets, about 16 cookies per sheet. Press the dough down just slightly and sprinkle with some of the additional salt. Place the baking sheets onto the center and upper racks of the oven and bake until golden brown but still soft, 13 to 15 minutes, rotating the baking sheets once while baking. Remove the cookies from the oven and cool on a baking rack before serving.

Makes 32 (3-inch) cookies.

CARROT CUPCAKES WITH CREAM CHEESE FROSTING AND CANDIED CARROTS

We serve these when there are children at the lodge—of any age. Mandy likes to create an event called the "Ice Cream Social" where guests are treated to a buffet of delicious desserts and these cupcakes are often present. Carrots grow well in the garden and we always have many beautiful varieties.

For the Carrot Cupcakes

3 CUPS PEELED AND SHREDDED CARROTS

4 LARGE EGGS

1½ CUPS GRANULATED SUGAR

1 CUP CANOLA OIL

1½ CUPS ALL-PURPOSE FLOUR

1½ TEASPOONS BAKING POWDER

1 TEASPOON BAKING SODA

½ TEASPOON SALT

½ TEASPOON GROUND GINGER

¼ TEASPOON GROUND CARDAMOM

½ TEASPOON GROUND CINNAMON

For the Cream Cheese Frosting

1 CUP (2 STICKS) UNSALTED BUTTER

1 CUP (8 OUNCES) CREAM CHEESE, SOFTENED

3 CUPS POWDERED SUGAR

1 TEASPOON PURE VANILLA EXTRACT

1 TEASPOON ORANGE ZEST

TO MAKE THE CUPCAKES: Preheat the oven to 325°F. This recipe fills 18 standard muffin cups. Depending on the size of your muffin tins, there might be batter left over or empty cups. Grease or line the muffin cups.

In a medium mixing bowl, whisk together the carrots, eggs, sugar, and oil. In another small mixing bowl, whisk together the flour, baking powder, baking soda, salt, ginger, cardamom, and cinnamon. Combine the flour mixture into the carrot mixture until both are well combined.

Divide the batter amongst the muffin cups, filling each about three-quarters full. If you have any muffin cups unfilled, put a little water in them. This helps protect the tin.

Bake the cupcakes for 25 minutes or until the cake is firm in the center. Cool the cupcakes completely before removing them.

Makes 18 cupcakes.

TO MAKE THE FROSTING: Combine the butter, cream cheese, powdered sugar, vanilla extract, and orange zest into a medium mixing bowl. Using an electric hand mixer, whip the mixture until it is light and fluffy.

Keep the frosting at room temperature before spreading or piping it onto the cooled cupcakes.

Makes 4 cups frosting.

For the Candied Carrots

I CUP GRANULATED SUGAR

I CUP WATER

I LARGE CARROT

FOR THE CANDIED CARROTS

You can grate the carrot and achieve the same end with the result being a small nest of candied carrot on top of the cupcake.

TO CANDY THE CARROTS: Bring the sugar and water to a boil in a small saucepan. Reduce to a low simmer. Peel the outside of the carrot. Then, peel the carrot lengthwise into long strips with a flat vegetable peeler. Drop the carrot strips into the sugar water. Simmer the carrot chips for about 15 minutes. Remove the carrots from the liquid using a mesh strainer. Dry the carrots onto a paper towel. Curl the carrots around a chopstick or a small dowel. Let them air-dry until they are dried completely.

Makes 15 to 30 curls depending on the size of the carrot.

TO SERVE: Top each frosted cupcake with a small candied piece of carrot.

HOT-SMOKED SALMON CROQUE MADAME WITH BÉCHAMEL SAUCE

Espelette is a Basque ground red pepper that Mandy prefers to cook with but other ground red pepper will do. These sandwiches are always a huge hit.

For the Béchamel Sauce

1 TABLESPOON UNSALTED BUTTER

1 TABLESPOON ALL-PURPOSE FLOUR

1 CUP WHOLE MILK

1 SPRIG THYME

SALT AND FRESHLY GROUND
    BLACK PEPPER

1 PINCH ESPELETTE PEPPER

For the Croque Madame

5 TABLESPOONS UNSALTED
    BUTTER

1 CLOVE GARLIC, SLICED THIN

8 SLICES THICK-CUT SOUR-
    DOUGH BREAD

2 TABLESPOONS DIJON MUSTARD

1½ CUPS GRATED GRUYÈRE CHEESE

4 THICK-CUT SLICES OF HAM

8 OUNCES HOT-SMOKED SALMON

4 LARGE EGGS

SALT AND FRESHLY GROUND
    BLACK PEPPER

TO MAKE THE SAUCE: Melt the butter into a medium saucepan over medium heat. Whisk in the flour and cook until the flour is golden yellow. Gradually whisk in the milk and the thyme sprig. Cook, stirring until the mixture comes just to a boil and has thickened. Remove from the heat. Season with salt, pepper, and the espelette. Set aside.

TO MAKE THE CROQUE MADAME: Preheat the oven to 375°F.

In a small saucepan, melt the butter and garlic slices together over medium heat just until simmering.

Using a pastry brush, brush all sides of the sourdough bread with the garlic butter. Reserve 3 teaspoons of the garlic butter for frying the eggs later. Spread the mustard on 4 of the slices of bread and then top with a tablespoon of the Gruyère cheese. Add on a slice of ham and a little smoked salmon. Top off the salmon with another tablespoon of cheese.

Heat a large ovenproof sauté pan over medium heat. Place the sandwiches in the pan and cook until golden brown. Spread 2 tablespoons of the béchamel sauce on top of each sandwich. Sprinkle a tablespoon more cheese on top and place the sauté pan in the oven until the sauce is golden brown and the cheese is completely melted.

Meanwhile, heat a small nonstick sauté pan over medium heat. Put a teaspoon of the remaining melted garlic butter into the preheated pan. Fry the eggs one at a time to desired doneness. Season with salt and pepper. Place one egg on top of each sandwich and serve.

Makes 4 servings.

SOURDOUGH PANZANELLA

This is our basic bread salad recipe we use all summer long. We love plenty of vinegar, garlic, and pepper in our mixture. And, of course, we use pungent sourdough bread. We top our salads with smoked halibut or salmon.

1 RUSTIC-STYLE SOURDOUGH BOULE, HAND TORN INTO ½-INCH PIECES

SALT AND FRESHLY GROUND BLACK PEPPER

⅓ CUP EXTRA-VIRGIN OLIVE OIL

3 TABLESPOONS APPLE CIDER VINEGAR

1 CLOVE GARLIC, PEELED AND MINCED

1 POUND ASSORTED SMALL HEIR-LOOM TOMATOES, QUARTERED

1 SMALL CUCUMBER, QUARTERED LENGTHWISE AND THINLY SLICED CROSSWISE

1 YELLOW BELL PEPPER, CUT INTO ¼-INCH DICE

½ CUP PICKLED RED ONIONS (SEE PAGE 215)

½ POUND MOZZARELLA, CUT INTO ½-INCH CUBES

¼ CUP TORN BASIL LEAVES

1 TABLESPOON MINCED TARRAGON

1 TABLESPOON TORN MINT LEAVES

3 CUPS MIXED GARDEN LETTUCES, WASHED AND DRIED

¼ CUP TOASTED PINE NUTS

Preheat the oven to 325°F.

Place the bread onto a baking sheet and sprinkle it liberally with salt and pepper. Put the baking sheet into the oven and toast the bread for about 10 minutes. Set aside.

In a large mixing bowl, whisk together the oil, vinegar, garlic, and some additional salt and pepper.

Add the tomatoes, cucumber, yellow pepper, pickled red onion, mozzarella, basil, tarragon, and mint. Toss well. Add in the garden greens and lightly toss. Before serving, add in the bread cubes and toss to coat. Add the pine nuts before serving.

Makes 6 servings.

TUTKA BAY SEAFOOD PAELLA WITH SUMMER SOFRITO

We've been lucky enough to work with several Spanish chefs at Tutka Bay Lodge who have taught me much about Spanish cuisine. We have an enormous paella pan that we bring down to the large deck and place onto the barbecue grill. The seafood can vary depending on market availability.

For the Summer Sofrito

2 TABLESPOONS PURE OLIVE OIL

I BUNCH GREEN ONION, WHITE AND LIGHT GREEN PART ONLY, CHOPPED

I SMALL YELLOW ONION, PEELED AND CHOPPED

I MEDIUM RED BELL PEPPER, HALVED, CORED, AND CHOPPED

I LARGE TOMATO, CORED AND CHOPPED

I SMALL BUNCH CILANTRO, CHOPPED

SALT AND FRESHLY GROUND BLACK PEPPER

For the Tutka Bay Seafood Paella

4 TABLESPOONS PURE OLIVE OIL

½ POUND SKINLESS BONELESS CHICKEN THIGHS

SALT AND FRESHLY GROUND BLACK PEPPER

½ POUND FRESH MIXED MUSHROOMS

I SMALL YELLOW ONION, PEELED, QUARTERED, AND SLICED

2 CLOVES GARLIC, PEELED AND MINCED

I CUP BOMBA OR OTHER SHORT-GRAIN RICE

SOFRITO

There are many variations of sofrito, some cooked, some raw. We vary our recipe often adding in hot peppers, green bell peppers, and other aromatics. This is a combination we prefer for paella.

TO MAKE THE SOFRITO: Put all the ingredients into a food processor. Pulse a few times until the mixture is finely diced and blended together.

Makes about I cup sofrito.

TO MAKE THE PAELLA: Heat 2 tablespoons of the oil in a large (14-inch) skillet or paella pan over medium-high heat. Rub the chicken with salt and pepper. Sauté the chicken in the skillet until it is browned, about 5 minutes. Set aside in a large mixing bowl.

In the same skillet, pour in a little additional oil and sauté the mushrooms, onion, and garlic until they are tender, 4 to 5 minutes. Transfer the vegetables to the same bowl as the chicken.

2 CUPS STORE-BOUGHT OR HOME-
MADE ONE-HOUR CHICKEN STOCK
(SEE PAGE 60)

1 CUP SUMMER SOFRITO

1 TEASPOON SMOKED PAPRIKA

1 LARGE PINCH SAFFRON

½ POUND ALASKA SIDESTRIPE OR
OTHER SHRIMP

½ POUND KING OR DUNGENESS
CRAB

½ POUND MUSSELS (OPTIONAL)

1 SMALL BUNCH FLAT-LEAF PARSLEY,
STEMMED AND CHOPPED

Place a tablespoon of oil in the same skillet and add in the rice. Stir a minute to coat the grains of rice. Add in ½ cup of chicken stock, the sofrito, paprika, and saffron. Bring the mixture to a simmer. Season to taste with salt and pepper.

Reduce the heat to medium-low. Add in the chicken and vegetable mixture. Drizzle ½ cup chicken stock over the mixture. Simmer about 6 to 8 minutes. Drizzle in another ½ cup chicken stock over the mixture. Simmer 6 to 8 minutes longer. You might have to add in a little bit more chicken stock but cook until the rice is tender. Arrange the shrimp, crab, and mussels (if using) atop the paella. Cook an additional 5 minutes. Sprinkle with parsley.

Makes 4 servings.

SALMON CROQUETTES

We can never make enough of these when they are on the menu. Sometimes we serve them over a salad as a luncheon item or on their own at the bar appetizer hour along with a little aioli combined with a touch of hot pepper sauce.

1 POUND RED SALMON

2 TABLESPOONS AIOLI (SEE PAGE 207)

2 TEASPOONS LEMON JUICE

1 TEASPOON DIJON MUSTARD

1 TABLESPOON CHOPPED PARSLEY

1 TABLESPOON CHOPPED TARRAGON

1 TABLESPOON CHOPPED CHIVES

¼ CUP FINELY CHOPPED GREEN ONIONS

2 TABLESPOONS SHREDDED PARMESAN CHEESE

½ TEASPOON MINCED GARLIC

2 CUPS PANKO

4 CUPS CANOLA OIL FOR FRYING

COARSE SEA SALT

Place the salmon in a food processer and blend until the flesh is lightly puréed.

Add in the aioli, lemon juice, mustard, parsley, tarragon, chives, green onion, Parmesan cheese, and garlic. Roll the mixture into 16 (1-ounce) balls (about the size of golf balls).

Place the panko in a shallow pan. Roll the balls in the panko and chill for 5 minutes.

Heat the oil in a large pot over medium heat to 365°F and fry each ball until the salmon is just cooked. Remove the croquettes from the oil with a mesh strainer and set on paper towels to drain. Season with sea salt.

Makes 16 croquettes.

SPOT SHRIMP PIZZA WITH WHITE SAUCE

We often prepare pizza for guests and staff. We cook the pizza in the oven as in this recipe or throw it onto the grill on the big deck. If you don't have a grill, We find a stovetop cast-iron grill pan handy for grilling small items like lemon slices.

COARSE CORNMEAL, FOR DUSTING

1 TABLESPOON UNSALTED BUTTER

1 TABLESPOON BREAD FLOUR

¾ CUP WHOLE MILK

2 CLOVES GARLIC, PEELED AND MINCED

½ CUP GRATED GRUYÈRE CHEESE

SALT AND FRESHLY GROUND BLACK PEPPER

1 TABLESPOONS PURE OLIVE OIL

1½ POUNDS SPOT SHRIMP, PEELED

1 POUND PIZZA DOUGH (SEE PAGE 215)

1 LEMON, SLICED AND GRILLED

1 CUP BABY ARUGULA

Preheat the oven to 475°F. Line a 13-by-18-inch baking sheet with parchment paper. Sprinkle the parchment paper with cornmeal.

Melt the butter in a small saucepan. Add in the flour and whisk for 1 minute. Slowly whisk in the milk and garlic. Continue to cook over medium heat until the mixture is thickened. Add in the Gruyère, mixing over low heat until the sauce is smooth. Season to taste with the salt and pepper.

Heat the oil in a large sauté pan. Season the shrimp with salt and pepper. Sear over high heat until the shrimp are cooked halfway through. Set aside.

Place the dough onto the prepared baking sheet. Stretch the dough out and press it toward the edges of the baking sheet. Pinch around the edges to make them slightly thicker than the rest of the crust.

Spread the white sauce onto the pizza. Add the shrimp and lemon slices evenly onto the sauce.

Bake the pizza for 10 to 15 minutes until golden brown. Remove from the oven and sprinkle with the arugula.

Makes 1 (12-inch) pizza.

RED CURRANT JAM TART

Red currant jam is worthy of becoming a staple in your pantry. There are several high-quality commercial brands available. We make this tart often in the summer and winter.

1 CUP CHOPPED WALNUTS

2 CUPS ALL-PURPOSE FLOUR

⅔ CUP GRANULATED SUGAR

¾ CUP (1½ STICKS) UNSALTED BUTTER

2 CUPS RED CURRANT JAM, HOMEMADE OR STORE-BOUGHT

Preheat the oven to 350°F. Grease two 9-by-1-inch fluted tart pans with removable bottoms.

Combine the walnuts, flour, sugar, and butter into the bowl of a food processor, pulsing until the mixture is finely ground. Use your hands to press the mixture into both tart pans to form the crusts. Bake the tart shells for 7 to 8 minutes or until the shells are just lightly golden around the edges.

Pour 1 cup of the red currant jam into each shell and smooth out the top using an off-set spatula. Bake an additional 2 minutes. Let set up overnight at room temperature before cutting.

Makes 2 (9-inch) tarts.

RHUBARB AND RICOTTA CHURROS

These are delicious treats to serve alongside little pots of melted chocolate or with ice cream.

CANOLA OIL FOR FRYING

¼ CUP GRANULATED SUGAR

I TEASPOON GROUND CINNAMON

I CUP WATER

2 TABLESPOONS LIGHT BROWN SUGAR

½ TEASPOON SALT

⅓ CUP UNSALTED BUTTER

I CUP BREAD FLOUR

2 LARGE EGGS

I CUP CHOPPED RHUBARB

¼ CUP FRESH RICOTTA CHEESE (SEE PAGE 212)

½ TEASPOON PURE VANILLA EXTRACT

I TEASPOON LEMON ZEST

Preheat the oil in a heavy, high-sided casserole to 375°F.

In a medium mixing bowl, mix the granulated sugar and cinnamon and set aside.

In a medium saucepan bring the water, brown sugar, salt, and butter to a boil. Remove the pan from the heat and add in the flour. Mix until well blended. Add in the eggs one at a time until fully incorporated. Add in the rhubarb, ricotta, vanilla, and lemon zest.

Spoon the batter into a piping bag with a medium round tip or a zipper storage bag with a ½-inch hole snipped from one corner.

When the oil is heated, squeeze some batter into the oil about 4 inches long. You should be able to cook 4 to 5 churros at a time. Cook them about a minute and turn them over with a slotted spoon.

Remove the churros with the slotted spoon and place them on a plate lined with paper towels to absorb any excess grease.

While still warm, roll each churro into the dish with the sugar and cinnamon mixture until coated.

Makes 24 (4-inch) churros.

WE GATHER THE OYSTERS AND THE WINE

FÊTE

Every day at 6:00 P.M., we serve drinks and appetizers in the main lodge or out on one of our decks. This is an hour-long party preceding dinner. It is a fantastic gathering of diverse and interesting people coming together to share the adventures of the day, talk about wine, the appetizers we're serving, and all things Alaska. It's the most festive and fascinating social time of the day at the lodge. Friends are made, families are strengthened, and romance is kindled.

For a perfect fête, we bring together intriguing wines, beers, a small collection of hard alcohol drinks, and appetizers that complement them. We consider approximately 2 to 3 drinks per person for our hour-long party. A 750-milliliter bottle of wine holds five 5-ounce servings. A liter bottle holds ten glasses. A bottle of Champagne serves six 4-ounce servings. We usually prepare 2 to 3 servings of appetizers per person. It's preferable to have a pound of ice available for each guest served.

Our seasonal and oft-changing wine selections have always been inspired by our experiences. Sometimes a wine invokes a memory of a trip or special event. Sometimes we have connected with the winery and winemaker in a personal way. And, certainly I go through phases—I think I was on a pinot noir "intensive" for several years. We offer our guests complimentary wine at the lodge, and each day we pair custom selections with appetizers and a curated cheese selection.

WINE AND FOOD PAIRINGS

Sauvignon blanc
The most widely served wine throughout the summer. Pairs well with pine nuts, oysters, scallops, citrus, cilantro, green apple, fish and chips, pizza, crab cakes, sashimi. We pair sauvignon blanc with goat cheeses and luxurious triple crèmes.

Chardonnay
Pairs well with almonds, halibut, shrimp, crab, tarragon, basil, apple, and squash. Oaked chardonnay goes quite nicely with smoked salmon, little omelets, fish cakes. We pair chardonnay with sharp aged Cheddar and Comté cheese.

Riesling
Pairs well with candied walnuts, smoked sausage, duck, rosemary, ginger, rhubarb chutney, curried scallops, sushi, and cranberries. We pair Riesling with goat cheese and blue cheeses.

Champagne
Pairs well with almost everything we serve during the appetizer hour! Champagne is particularly delicious with our crab cakes and scallops, and Indian appetizers. We pair Champagne with goat cheese and triple crèmes.

Pinot Noir
Pairs well with walnuts, lamb, sausage, dried fruit, strawberries, Alaska salmon, mushrooms. We pair pinot noir with Époisses and Manchego.

garden, ½ cup Cointreau, and 2 cups vodka. Serve over ice.

Gin

Mix 2 cups gin, 1 handful of whole blackberries from the garden, 1 handful of torn basil leaves from the garden, ½ cup sugar, 1 cup lime juice, 1 cup club soda, and 1 tablespoon crème de cassis.

Bourbon

Mix 2 cups bourbon, 2 cups cranberry liqueur, 2 cups fresh lemon juice, and 1 cup simple syrup (one part sugar, one part water). Pour over ice and garnish with a cranberry cluster.

Scotch

Combine 2 cups sparkling apple cider with ½ cup blended Scotch. Serve with a small cluster of red currants and ice and a sliced apple on top.

Tequila

Combine 2 cups orange juice and 1 cup tequila. Add in ¼ cup raspberry concentrate and garnish with an orange slice.

Cabernet Sauvignon

Pairs well with walnuts, tomatoes, rosemary, barbecued meats, cranberries, and empanadas. We pair cabernet sauvignon with aged Cheddars, Parmigiano-Reggiano, and Gorgonzola.

THE CHEESE BOARD

We could write an entire book just on the cheeses we serve at Tutka Bay Lodge. We have a small refrigerator behind the bar dedicated to cheese only. We monitor and freshly wrap our cheeses daily. We almost always serve two hot appetizers and a couple of cold items during our appetizer hour. The star of our collection, however, is the cheese board. We serve our cheeses before dinner, not between the entrée and dessert as I learned to do in France. An advantage: guests come in to the lodge from hiking and

THE LIQUOR CABINET

We don't keep a deep collection of hard alcohol on hand but always stock the usual offerings. We often feature the following cocktails during our appetizer hour, each offered with a little Alaska twist.

Vodka

Combine 2 sliced lemons, 2 sliced limes, 1 cup whole blueberries from the trail by the cooking school, 1 cup crushed mint leaves from the exploring and they are hungry. Their palates are receptive to different flavors and textures.

One small pleasure we have every year before summer gets started is to sit down and select our seasonal collection of cheeses. We start by listening carefully to our cheesemonger's recommendations, trying samples, and thinking about what works with our appetizer and wine list. Classically, a cheese course represents at least three different cheeses, one of each type of milk: cow, sheep, or goat.

Here are a few tips for a successful cheese board:

* *Choose a nice board to serve your cheese on. I like the newer style bamboo cutting boards for cheese service. They are too pretty and too soft to actually cut on but perfect for serving food.*

* *Bring cheese to room temperature before serving for best flavor.*

* *Serve a different small knife for each type of cheese (so one knife isn't used on multiple cheeses).*

* *Rather than organizing cheese by the classic three milk types, you could pick a theme for your cheese (that will complement your other appetizers and wine selection as well). An example is serving only cheeses from Italy or a collection of American blue cheeses.*

* *Don't cut cheese into individual portions. Serve them in chunky wedges or blocks. That helps to increase the longevity of the cheese.*

* *Cheese is a complex and ever-changing topic. Keep a small notebook and take notes (even photos) of cheeses you enjoy.*

We like to add specialty fruit and nut breads we make daily in the kitchen to our cheese board. We also serve a small basket of plain baguettes or homemade crackers.

We make condiments and preserves such as blueberry chutney, pickled beets and onions, or hot and spicy pickles. A treasure every summer is the small amount of rose petal jam we can make from wild roses near the lodge.

A current favorite cheese we like to serve is Shropshire blue cheese. Serve Shropshire on a slice of chocolate walnut bread with a bit of blueberry chutney. Shropshire blue cheese is a cow's milk blue cheese made with vegetable rennet and annatto, a natural food coloring. The annatto adds a surprising orange color to the Shropshire, which has been called "Stilton colored with sunshine."

GRILLED OYSTERS WITH SALMON BACON AND PERNOD

You can use regular bacon for this recipe. We happen to like the salmon bacon we make and the flavors of fennel and Pernod together.

1 SMALL FENNEL, FRONDS AND STEM SEPARATED

1 SHALLOT, PEELED AND MINCED

2¾ CUPS FINE DRY BREADCRUMBS

½ CUP MINCED FRESH PARSLEY LEAVES, PLUS PARSLEY SPRIGS FOR GARNISH

3 GARLIC CLOVES, PEELED AND MINCED

½ CUP (1 STICK) UNSALTED BUTTER, MELTED

12 SLICES OF SALMON BACON WITH RHUBARB LACQUER (SEE PAGE 47)

¼ CUP PERNOD, DIVIDED

24 KACHEMAK BAY OYSTERS, SHUCKED, IN HALF-SHELL

COARSE SALT FOR FILLING THE PLATTERS

SEAWEED FOR GARNISH (IF AVAILABLE)

LEMON WEDGES FOR GARNISH

Heat the grill to a steady high heat.

Mince the fennel stem. Rough chop the fennel fronds. In a medium bowl combine the fennel, shallot, breadcrumbs, parsley, and garlic. Pour in the melted butter and stir until combined.

Crumble the salmon bacon. Pour 1 teaspoon of Pernod over each oyster, and then top with the bacon crumbles and the breadcrumb mixture.

Arrange the oysters on the grill and cook until the edges of the oysters begin to curl and the breadcrumbs are browned well.

Garnish the platters with the salt, seaweed, and lemon wedges.

Makes 24 appetizers.

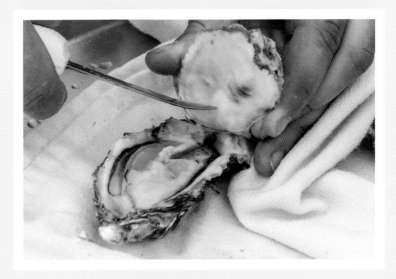

HALIBUT SLIDERS

We love to serve these little bites during our famous appetizer hour on the back deck. For much of the summer, hummingbirds fly around our heads and dart between the wine table and the appetizers. They are quite beautiful. This recipe calls for Peri Peri sauce (our favorite brand of South African hot sauce) but you can substitute your own favorite. We have a good barbecue sauce recipe in The Winterlake Lodge Cookbook.

1 POUND HALIBUT FILLET, SKINNED

1 LEMON, HALVED

SALT

1 SMALL BUNCH FLAT-LEAF PARSLEY, CLEANED, TRIMMED, AND DICED

1 CUP UNSEASONED FINE BREAD-CRUMBS, DIVIDED

½ YELLOW ONION, PEELED AND MINCED

1 TEASPOON OF PERI PERI (OR OTHER HOT PEPPER) SAUCE

2 TABLESPOONS CHOPPED GREEN ONIONS

2 TEASPOONS CHOPPED CILANTRO

1 LARGE EGG, BEATEN

2 TABLESPOONS AIOLI (SEE PAGE 207)

1 TABLESPOON UNSALTED BUTTER

4 TABLESPOONS PURE OLIVE OIL, DIVIDED

1 CUP BABY SPINACH, WASHED AND DRIED

4 MINI BRIOCHE SLIDER BUNS

4 TABLESPOONS BARBECUE SAUCE

Rinse and pat dry the fish.

Fill a medium saucepan with enough water to come up about 2 inches. Add ½ of the lemon, ¼ teaspoon salt, and half of the parsley. Bring the water to a simmer and add in the fish. Poach until done, about 5 to 7 minutes or until it flakes nicely with a fork. Remove the fish from the pan, flake apart completely, and set aside to cool.

In a large mixing bowl, combine the halibut, ½ cup of the breadcrumbs, the yellow onion, Peri Peri sauce, green onion, remaining parsley, cilantro, egg, and aioli. Gently mix the ingredients together until fully incorporated.

Shape the mixture into 8 patties. Dredge each one lightly in the remaining ½ cup of breadcrumbs. Refrigerate for 10 minutes to firm the patties up.

In a medium sauté pan melt the butter and 2 tablespoons of the olive oil over medium-low heat. Add in the cakes and cook until golden, 3 to 5 minutes per side.

Squeeze the remaining ½ lemon and drizzle the remaining 2 tablespoons olive oil over the spinach, Season the spinach with salt and pepper. Place the dressed baby spinach onto each slider bun, followed by a halibut patty and then top it off with homemade barbecue sauce.

Makes 8 sliders.

PAN-SEARED SCALLOPS WITH HONEY CIDER GLAZE

We use the jumbo, or weathervane, scallops for this recipe. One scallop fits nicely onto an appetizer-style spoon. We might add a little braised Swiss chard for presentation.

2 CUPS APPLE CIDER

½ SHALLOT, FINELY CHOPPED

FRESHLY GROUND BLACK PEPPER

¼ CUP HONEY

½ GREEN APPLE, DICED

2 TABLESPOONS UNSALTED
  BUTTER

4 TABLESPOONS CANOLA OIL

2 DOZEN WEATHERVANE
  SCALLOPS

SALT

Place the cider, shallot, a few twists of black pepper, honey, and green apple in a medium saucepan. Simmer this mixture until the liquid is reduced to a sauce consistency. This takes about 10 to 15 minutes. After the sauce has thickened, turn off the heat and set aside.

In a large, heavy sauté pan over high heat, melt the butter and the oil. Pat the scallops completely dry and season them with salt and pepper. Once the pan is very hot, add the scallops to the pan and sauté until cooked through.

When the scallops are just browned, turn off the heat and drizzle on the glaze, lightly coating the scallops. Divide the sauce and scallops among plates to serve.

Makes 24 appetizers.

RICE CAKES WITH SMOKED SALMON

We made a little video of Mandy demonstrating this recipe on YouTube. Check it out. We serve these appetizers at the bar year round and they are always well received.

For the Rice

1½ CUPS SHORT-GRAIN RICE

3 CUPS WATER

1 TABLESPOON RICE WINE VINEGAR

1 TABLESPOON MIRIN

1 TEASPOON GRATED LEMON ZEST

½ CUP FLAKED HOT-SMOKED (KIPPERED) SALMON

For the Toppings

¼ CUP HOT-SMOKED (KIPPERED) SALMON, FROZEN AND GRATED

1 (2-INCH) PIECE OF SALMON SKIN (SCALES REMOVED)

¼ CUP HONEY

¼ CUP PLUS 2 TABLESPOONS SOY SAUCE, DIVIDED

2 TABLESPOONS SHERRY VINEGAR

2 TABLESPOONS RICE WINE VINEGAR

¼ CUP MAYONNAISE

2 TABLESPOONS CHILE-GARLIC PASTE (SEE PAGE 66)

1 SMALL BUNCH SCALLION, CHOPPED

1 SMALL BUNCH CILANTRO, CHOPPED

For Assembly

RICE FLOUR FOR DREDGING

CANOLA OIL FOR FRYING

TO MAKE THE RICE: Line an 8-by-8-inch baking pan with plastic wrap, leaving enough extra plastic wrap to fold over the top later.

Combine the rice, water, rice wine vinegar, mirin, lemon zest, and flaked smoked salmon into a medium high-sided saucepan with a good fitting lid. Stir to combine all the ingredients. Bring the mixture to a boil and then reduce the heat to a simmer. Cook for about 15 minutes until the rice has absorbed all the liquid and the grains are tender. Let the rice cool for another 15 minutes.

Firmly press the cooled rice into the prepared baking pan, using water-moistened hands to prevent sticking. Press the plastic wrap over the top of the rice and refrigerate for about 2 hours or overnight.

TO MAKE THE TOPPINGS: Preheat the oven to 300°F.

Place the grated frozen smoked salmon and the salmon skin onto a non-stick baking sheet. Place the baking sheet into the oven and bake for about 15 minutes, or until crispy and browned but not burned.

MAKE THE HONEY-SOY DRIZZLE: Combine the honey, ¼ cup soy sauce, sherry vinegar, and rice wine vinegar. Mix together and set aside.

MAKE THE SPICY MAYONNAISE: Combine the mayonnaise, chile-garlic paste, and 2 tablespoons of soy sauce.

TO ASSEMBLE: Cut the chilled and firmed rice into 1-by-2 inch rectangles, keeping the knife moistened with water to prevent sticking. Dredge the rice cakes in the rice flour.

Heat the oil in a medium high-sided saucepan, deep enough to just about cover the rectangles. Bring the temperature to 360°F. Fry the rice cakes for about 5 minutes until they are golden brown. Drain on paper towels.

Paint each rice cake with a little bit of the honey-soy drizzle. We actually use a small paintbrush we keep in the kitchen for this purpose but you can use a fork as well. Top each cake with a dollop of the spicy mayonnaise, a bit of smoked salmon, a bit of scallion, and cilantro.

Makes 32 rice cakes.

BULLWHIP KELP SWEET AND SPICY PICKLES

The first time we made these, we didn't wash the kelp well enough and the results were too pungent to eat. Look for small, young kelp and soak the stipes well right before you make your pickles. Stipe is the name for the O-shaped stem of the kelp. Peel the stipe with a vegetable peeler.

3 CUPS WHITE VINEGAR

3 CUPS GRANULATED SUGAR

2 TEASPOONS CELERY SEED

1 BAY LEAF

1 TABLESPOON WHOLE ALLSPICE

2 TABLESPOONS MUSTARD SEED

2 TEASPOONS RED PEPPER FLAKES

1 TEASPOON TURMERIC

8 CUPS BULLWHIP KELP STIPE, WASHED, PEELED, AND CUT INTO ½-INCH CHUNKS

1 RED ONION, PEELED AND CUT IN HALF, SLICED THINLY

2 GARLIC CLOVES, PEELED AND HALVED

1 TABLESPOON BLACK PEPPERCORNS

Sterilize 6 half-pint canning jars, lids, and rings by immersing them in boiling water for 15 minutes.

Combine the vinegar, sugar, celery seed, bay leaf, allspice, mustard seed, pepper flakes, and the turmeric into a large saucepan over high heat. Bring to a boil and reduce the heat. Add in the kelp, onion, and garlic. Simmer over low heat for about 1 hour. Strain the mixture, reserving the brine.

Pack the kelp chunks, onion, and garlic into half-pint canning jars. Add in the peppercorns. Pour the hot brine over the kelp, keeping a ½-inch space at the top of the jar.

Wipe the top rims of the filled jars with a clean cloth or paper towel. Place the prepared lids and rings on the jars.

Seal the jars using the boiling water canning method.

Makes 6 half-pint jars of pickles.

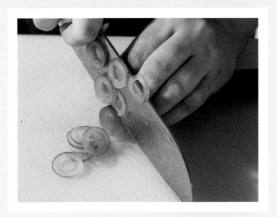

CHARRED TOMATO FLATBREAD

If you have a stovetop or other grill, you may prefer to char the tomatoes there rather than a broiler. Favorite herbs we use on flatbread are flat-leaf parsley, thyme, dill, chervil, and basil.

1 CUP MULTICOLORED CHERRY TOMATOES, SLICED IN HALF

1 CUP EXTRA-VIRGIN OLIVE OIL, DIVIDED

SALT

ALL-PURPOSE FLOUR FOR DUSTING

1 POUND PIZZA DOUGH (SEE PAGE 215)

3 GARLIC CLOVES, MINCED

½ RED ONION, PEELED AND SLICED

¼ YELLOW ONION, PEELED AND SLICED

3 SPRIGS FRESH THYME

FRESHLY GROUND BLACK PEPPER

COARSE CORNMEAL, FOR DUSTING

4 TABLESPOONS GOAT CHEESE

¼ CUP SHREDDED MANCHEGO CHEESE

1 CUP BABY ARUGULA

½ CUP MIXED FRESH HERBS

Preheat the oven to 400°F. Line a 13-by-18-inch baking sheet with parchment paper.

Turn the oven broiler on high and place the tomatoes onto the baking sheet. Sprinkle the tomatoes with some olive oil and salt. Place the baking sheet under the broiler and broil for 3 minutes. Watch the tomatoes carefully. Once they brown slightly, flip them over and roast the other side. Remove the tomatoes from the oven and slide the parchment paper off from the baking sheet. Set the tomatoes aside.

On a floured cutting board, cut the pizza dough in half and gently press each piece into a thin 3-by-12-inch oval.

Combine ½ cup of the olive oil, garlic, and the red and yellow onions into a sauté pan. Cook until the onions are soft and translucent, about 8 minutes. Remove the pan from the heat and add in the thyme. Season with salt and pepper to taste.

Line the baking sheet with another sheet of parchment. Dust the baking sheet lightly with the cornmeal. Place the flatbreads down and brush them generously with olive oil.

Top the dough with some of the charred tomatoes and scatter each with some goat cheese, Manchego cheese, and the onion mixture.

Bake the flatbreads in the oven for 8 to 10 minutes, or until the dough bubbles and the crust is golden brown.

Top the flatbreads with the arugula and mixed herbs before cutting and serving.

Makes 2 (12-inch) flatbreads.

ROCKFISH FRITTERS

We might call this fish fritters as we could use any number of other Alaska fish. Rockfish is a pride and joy of our region and we love highlighting all the different species we have access to in many of our recipes.

4 SMALL RED POTATOES

EXTRA-VIRGIN OLIVE OIL

I CLOVE GARLIC, MINCED

I BUNCH GREEN ONIONS, MINCED

½ YELLOW ONION, PEELED, HALVED, AND MINCED

I CUP WHOLE MILK

I POUND ROCKFISH, BONED AND SKINNED

SALT AND FRESHLY GROUND BLACK PEPPER

GROUND NUTMEG

I LEMON, CUT IN HALF

I SMALL BUNCH FLAT-LEAF PARSLEY, MINCED

CANOLA OIL FOR FRYING

2 LARGE EGGS

I CUP ALL-PURPOSE FLOUR

I CUP PANKO

COARSE SEA SALT (OPTIONAL)

CREAMY HORSERADISH DIPPING SAUCE (SEE PAGE 116)

Heat a medium stockpot with water and bring to a boil. Wash the potatoes and quarter them. Boil the potatoes until they are tender, about 8 to 10 minutes. Drain and place the potatoes into a medium mixing bowl.

Heat 2 tablespoons of olive oil in a sauté pan. Add in the garlic, green onions, and yellow onion. Sauté over low heat until the onion is soft and translucent, about 8 to 10 minutes. Add in the milk. Bring the mixture to a simmer. Cut the fish up into pieces that fit easily into your pan. Add the fish into the milk mixture. Poach the fish for about 5 to 7 minutes.

Lift the fish out of the milk mixture and place it in the bowl with the potatoes. Season the potatoes and fish with salt and pepper. Add in a few gratings of nutmeg, the juice of ½ lemon, and the parsley. Mix the mixture lightly. You can vary the texture of the batter here either by blending well or leaving it a little chunky. Add in 1 egg and mix well. Refrigerate the fish mixture for about 30 minutes.

In the meantime, bring the deep fryer up to 360°F.

Crack the other egg into a small mixing bowl and mix with a fork. Place the flour and panko separately into 2 small mixing bowls.

Shape about 1 ounce of the fish batter into a round ball. Dip the ball into the flour, then the egg, and finally the panko. Repeat with as many balls as you want to make. Drop 1 fish ball into the fryer to check the temperature. It will take about 2 to 3 minutes to cook, turning a light golden brown. Repeat.

Cut the remaining ½ lemon into wedges. Sprinkle the rockfish fritters with chunky sea salt if you prefer and serve with our Creamy Horseradish Dipping Sauce (see page 116) and lemon wedges.

Makes 24 fritters.

CREAMY HORSERADISH DIPPING SAUCE

This pungent sauce can be used during appetizer hour for many different bites.

1 CUP SOUR CREAM

JUICE OF ½ LEMON

¼ CUP GRATED HORSERADISH

1 CLOVE GARLIC, PEELED AND MINCED

1 TABLESPOON DIJON MUSTARD

1 TEASPOON RED WINE VINEGAR

2 TEASPOONS CHOPPED CHIVES

SALT AND FRESHLY GROUND BLACK PEPPER

Place the sour cream, lemon juice, horseradish, garlic, mustard, vinegar, and chives into a medium mixing bowl. Whisk until the mixture is smooth and creamy. Season with salt and pepper to taste. Place in the refrigerator for at least 4 hours or overnight to allow flavors to meld. Sauce can be stored in the refrigerator in an airtight container for 2 to 3 weeks.

Makes 1 cup sauce.

SALMON PIEROGI

The Russian heritage communities near Tutka Bay Lodge inspire us but the inspiration for these came from a visit to a small shop near Pike Place Market in Seattle. We travel to Seattle often and like to stay near this area. We always find ourselves in the long line at the pierogi shop. We use a small deep fryer to prepare these but we included instructions for frying them in a saucepan. The pastries can be steamed or boiled as well.

For the Dough

3 CUPS ALL-PURPOSE FLOUR (PLUS EXTRA FOR DUSTING)

¼ TEASPOON SALT

1 TABLESPOON BAKING POWDER

3 LARGE EGGS

1 CUP SOUR CREAM

For the Filling

1½ CUPS SAUERKRAUT, DRAINED, RINSED, DRIED, AND CHOPPED

1 YELLOW ONION, DICED, DIVIDED

5 TABLESPOONS UNSALTED BUTTER, DIVIDED

1 CUP STORE-BOUGHT OR HOME-MADE ONE-HOUR CHICKEN STOCK (SEE PAGE 60)

SALT AND FRESHLY GROUND BLACK PEPPER

4 RED POTATOES, BOILED AND CUT INTO ¼-INCH DICE

1 POUND RED SALMON, SKINNED AND BONED, CUT INTO ¼-INCH CUBES

CANOLA OIL FOR FRYING

TO MAKE THE DOUGH: Combine the flour, salt, and baking powder into a small mixing bowl. In a separate small mixing bowl, beat the eggs and sour cream until smooth and well combined. Combine the flour mixture to the sour cream mixture.

Knead the dough for about 5 minutes on a floured surface. Cover the dough and let it rest for an hour at room temperature.

Roll the dough out to ⅛-inch thickness on a floured surface. Using a 3-inch round cutter, create 12 circles of dough.

TO MAKE THE FILLING: In a sauté pan over medium heat, sauté the sauerkraut and half the onion in 2 tablespoons of butter until the onion is translucent, about 6 to 8 minutes. Use a bit of chicken stock for moisture as needed. Season the mixture with salt and pepper to taste. Set aside.

In a medium sauté pan, sauté the remaining onion in 3 tablespoons of butter until soft and translucent. Add in the potatoes and the salmon chunks. Season with salt and pepper. Cook the mixture until warmed through and the salmon is just cooked through. When both the sauerkraut and potato mixtures are cooled, combine them.

TO ASSEMBLE: Spoon 1 to 2 tablespoons of the sauerkraut-potato mixture onto each circle. This amount can vary depending on how finely chopped the vegetables and seafood are. Fold the dough over to make a half-moon shape and press the edges down to seal with a fork.

Place enough canola oil into a medium-high sided saucepan to about 3 inches deep. Heat the canola oil to 360°F and fry the pierogi for 3 to 5 minutes, or until they float to the top and are golden brown. Using a strainer, drain the pierogi onto paper towels. Serve with our Creamy Horseradish Dipping Sauce (see page 116).

Makes 12 (3-inch) pierogi.

ROSTI CRAB CAKES WITH FENNEL RÉMOULADE

This is a cross between shredded potatoes and traditional crab cakes. It's a nice change from the usual. We serve this with a vibrant fennel rémoulade.

For the Rosti Crab Cakes

2 CLOVES GARLIC, CRUSHED

2 LARGE RUSSET POTATOES

8 OUNCES DUNGENESS LUMP
   CRABMEAT

1 TABLESPOON FRESH LEMON JUICE

2 FINELY CHOPPED CHIVES

1½ TABLESPOONS CHOPPED FRESH
   CILANTRO

1 TEASPOON CHILE-GARLIC PASTE
   (SEE PAGE 66)

SALT AND FRESHLY GROUND
   BLACK PEPPER

CANOLA OIL FOR SEARING

CLARIFIED BUTTER FOR SEARING
   (SEE PAGE 208)

FENNEL RÉMOULADE
   (SEE PAGE 210)

TO MAKE THE CRAB CAKES: Line a 13-by-18-inch baking sheet with parchment paper. Bring a large stockpot filled with salted water to a boil. Add in the garlic.

Scrub the potatoes, leave them unpeeled, and place them into the pot of garlic water. Par-cook the potatoes until they are just tender but not soft, about 8 to 10 minutes. Remove the potatoes from the water and discard the garlic. Chill the potatoes for 1 hour and set aside.

Meanwhile, place the crabmeat, lemon juice, chives, cilantro, and chile-garlic paste into a small mixing bowl and mix thoroughly.

When potatoes are cooled, grate the flesh on the largest hole of a box grater, pushing the potatoes all the way down the length of the grater so that the strips are as long as possible.

Carefully combine the grated potato and crab mixture, trying not to break up the potato. Season the potato-crab mixture with salt and pepper to taste. Form the mixture into 16 small cakes, shaping and pressing them together. Place the cakes onto the baking sheet, cover the cakes with plastic wrap, and place the baking sheet in the refrigerator for about an hour to chill and become firm.

To cook, heat 1 tablespoon of the oil and 1 tablespoon of the clarified butter in a 12-inch sauté pan until the oil is hot. Gently slide in half of the rosti crab cakes with a spatula. Turn the heat down to medium and cook for 3 minutes on each side. Repeat with the remaining crab cakes, adding in more oil and butter as necessary. Dollop each cake with some of the Fennel Rémoulade.

Makes 16 appetizers.

SEA LETTUCE RELISH

Sea lettuce is plentiful along ocean tidal lines all over the world. This dish is a delicious "little bite" and you can try market-available seaweed if you don't have access to sea lettuce. Sambal is an Asian chile sauce.

2 CUPS SEA LETTUCE

1 TABLESPOON SOY SAUCE

1 TEASPOON GRANULATED SUGAR

1 TABLESPOON SAKE

1 TABLESPOON RICE VINEGAR

1 TABLESPOON SESAME OIL

1 TEASPOON SAMBAL

1 CLOVE GARLIC, MINCED

1 TABLESPOON SESAME SEEDS,
  TOASTED

Rinse and soak the sea lettuce in cold water for at least 15 minutes. Dry carefully and chop. In a small mixing bowl, combine the soy sauce, sugar, sake, rice vinegar, sesame oil, sambal, garlic, and sesame seeds together to make a relish. Combine the sea lettuce and relish together.

Makes 2 cups relish.

DUNGENESS CRAB STEAMED BUNS

This recipe requires a steamer—either a traditional Chinese bamboo one or a metal one. You need to place something onto the steamer so the buns don't stick. We use parchment paper cut out to accommodate each bun, but you could use cabbage leaves. Serve this with our Dipping Sauce for the Chilli-Crab Fresh Rolls (see page 66)

For the Buns

1 PACKAGE (2½ TEASPOONS) ACTIVE
DRY YEAST

1 CUP WARM MILK (110°–115°F)

2½ CUPS ALL-PURPOSE FLOUR (PLUS
EXTRA FOR DUSTING)

½ CUP GRANULATED SUGAR

½ TEASPOON SALT

2½ TEASPOONS CANOLA OIL

For the Filling

1 RED BELL PEPPER

1 TEASPOON CANOLA OIL

½ POUND DUNGENESS LUMP CRAB-
MEAT, MINCED

1 TEASPOON SOY SAUCE

3 GREEN ONIONS, CHOPPED

1 CARROT, PEELED AND SHREDDED

2 CLOVES GARLIC, PEELED AND
MINCED

1 (1-INCH) KNOB GINGER, PEELED
AND GRATED

1 TEASPOON OYSTER SAUCE

1 TEASPOON HOT PEPPER SAUCE

SALT AND FRESHLY GROUND
BLACK PEPPER

TO MAKE THE BUNS: Dissolve the yeast in the warm milk.

In a large mixing bowl, combine the flour, sugar, and salt. Pour in the yeast-milk mixture and the oil. Stir and knead the dough until a ball is formed. Turn the dough out onto a floured work surface. Knead the dough for about 15 minutes, dusting the dough with flour if necessary. Cover the dough and let it rest in a warm place for about 30 minutes. Roll the dough out with a rolling pin, starting from the middle of the dough and working your way out. Roll the dough into a 12-by-18-inch rectangle. Brush the dough with a little water. Roll the dough up from the long edge into a log. The log should be 18 inches long. Cut the log into 12 pieces.

TO MAKE THE FILLING: Preheat the oven to broil.

Place the bell pepper onto a baking sheet and broil on the top rack of the oven, using tongs to turn it as each side blackens. Place the pepper in a small mixing bowl, cover it with plastic wrap, and allow it to cool for 20 minutes. Peel the skin off the pepper and discard the stem and seeds. Chop the pepper and set it aside.

Heat the oil in a wok or medium sauté pan over medium-high heat. Add in the crab, soy sauce, onions, carrot, garlic, ginger, oyster sauce, and hot sauce. Sauté for 2 to 3 minutes. Season with salt and pepper. Cool the filling.

TO ASSEMBLE: Roll each piece of dough out to a 3-inch disk. Take 1 disk and hold it in the palm of your hand. Place a large spoonful of the filling into the center of the round. Begin working your way around the circle pulling in an edge and crimping it to create a pleat. Do this around the entire bun. Gather the pleats together in the center and twist to seal.

Place the buns on a parchment-lined tray and then cover with plastic wrap. Let the buns rest at room temperature for 30 minutes.

Place a circular piece of oiled parchment underneath each bun. Place the buns onto the perforated rack of the steamer. Bring some water in the bottom of the steamer to a boil. Place the perforated rack over the steaming water and cover with a lid. Steam the buns for about 10 minutes.

Makes 12 buns.

QUICK FRUIT AND NUT BREAD

We serve this bread many ways, but we love to slather on a cream cheese-honey spread and fresh seasonal berries.

2 PACKAGES (5 TEASPOONS) ACTIVE
DRY YEAST

1¼ CUPS WATER, ROOM
TEMPERATURE

¼ CUP HONEY

2 TABLESPOONS WALNUT OIL

4 CUPS ALL-PURPOSE FLOUR

¾ CUP WHOLE-WHEAT FLOUR

1 TABLESPOON SALT

1 CUP MIXED DRIED FRUITS
(BLUEBERRIES, CHERRIES,
CRANBERRIES)

1 CUP TOASTED WALNUTS

Preheat oven to 350°F. Line a 13-by-18-inch baking sheet with parchment paper.

Into a small mixing bowl, place the yeast, water, honey, and walnut oil. In a large mixing bowl, combine the all-purpose flour, whole-wheat flour, and salt. Pour the wet ingredients into the flour mixture and combine thoroughly. Add in the dried fruit and nuts to the dough and mix for only a minute longer. Let the dough sit for 5 minutes covered in a warm area.

Shape the dough into two smaller baguette-style loafs. Place the dough onto the baking sheet and score the top of the dough with a knife to allow the bread to expand. Bake for 15 to 20 minutes.

Makes 2 (1-pound) loaves.

SHRIMP CHIPS

If you've ever feasted on those delicious salty, fishy multicolored Asian shrimp chips, this is the recipe. But, we use pristine fish and other fresh ingredients so you can munch away worry-free.

1 POUND RAW ALASKA SHRIMP, PEELED

1 (1-INCH) KNOB FRESH GINGER, PEELED AND GRATED

3¾ CUPS TAPIOCA FLOUR (PLUS EXTRA FOR KNEADING AND ROLLING)

2 TEASPOONS FINE SEA SALT

1 TEASPOON FRESHLY GROUND BLACK PEPPER

½ TEASPOON GRANULATED SUGAR

CANOLA OIL FOR DEEP FRYING

Place the shrimp and ginger into the bowl of a food processor. Pulse until the shrimp is puréed and very smooth. You might have to add a few drops of water if the shrimp becomes too thick to blend smoothly. Add in the flour, salt, pepper, and sugar.

Spread some tapioca flour onto a work surface. Remove the shrimp mixture from the food processor and place the dough onto the work surface. Knead the mixture lightly until it comes together enough to roll the dough into a cylindrical shape. You may wish to make two ½-pound logs depending on how big you want your shrimp chips to be.

Steam the shrimp logs (either in a proper steamer or on a rack set over briskly simmering water) for about 30 minutes. The logs will be a little rubbery and the color of the logs slightly darker.

Remove the logs from the steamer and chill completely, about 30 minutes. You can pop the logs in the freezer for about 10 minutes if you want to speed up the process. The shrimp logs should be completely firm and cooled before slicing.

Slice the log into paper-thin chips. The thinner the chips, the puffier they will be. Lay the chips out onto a baking sheet and air-dry for about 45 minutes. In Asia, the chips are often set out in the sun to dry.

Heat the canola oil to 375°F in a large pot or wok. Drop in a few chips at a time and remove them when they are completely puffed, just a minute or two. Drain the chips on paper towels. Serve the hot chips immediately or store them in an airtight container for a day or two.

Makes about 65 chips.

SPICY ROASTED CHICKPEA BEANS

We only use organic chickpea beans in our kitchen. They are easy to find in canned form these days.

2 (15-OUNCE) CANS CHICKPEA
   BEANS, DRAINED

4 TABLESPOONS PURE OLIVE OIL

1 TEASPOON DRIED GARLIC

1 TEASPOON SMOKED PAPRIKA

SALT AND FRESHLY GROUND
   BLACK PEPPER

½ TEASPOON CAYENNE PEPPER

Preheat the oven to 400°F. Line a 13-by-18-inch baking sheet with parchment.

Dry the chickpeas on a kitchen towel. Combine the olive oil, garlic, and paprika in a medium mixing bowl. Toss in the chickpeas and coat evenly. Season with salt and pepper to taste. Add in the cayenne pepper. Transfer the chickpea mixture to the baking sheet and spread out into a single layer.

Bake the chickpeas for about 30 minutes, stirring after 15 minutes.

Makes 2 cups chickpeas.

PUFF PASTRY FLATBREAD

We add our puff pastry flatbreads to luncheon or some dinner breadbaskets. You can cheat and purchase good-quality (meaning butter vs. oil) commercial puff pastry and create the same results. This recipe can go into your toolbox as a "quick puff pastry" recipe.

2 CUPS BREAD FLOUR (PLUS EXTRA FOR DUSTING)

1 TEASPOON SALT

1 CUP (2 STICKS) UNSALTED BUTTER, CHILLED

¼ CUP COLD WATER

CANOLA OIL FOR FRYING

2 SPRIGS OF THYME, PICKED

MEDIUM COARSE SALT FOR FINISHING

Sift the flour and salt into a large mixing bowl. Roughly break the butter into small chunks, add them to the bowl, and rub the flour and butter between your fingers.

Make a well in the bowl and pour in about ¼ cup of cold water, mixing until you have a firm rough dough, adding extra water as needed. Cover the dough and let it rest for about 20 minutes in the refrigerator.

Turn the dough out onto a lightly floured board, knead gently, and form into a smooth rectangle. Roll out the dough to about a 12-by-18-inch rectangle. Keep the edges straight and even.

Fold the top third down to the center, then the bottom third up and over that. Give the dough a quarter turn (to the left or right) and roll out again to three times the length. Fold as before, cover with plastic wrap, and chill for at least 20 minutes before rolling to use.

Roll out the dough to about ¼-inch thickness. Cut the dough into 3-by-4-inch rectangles.

Heat a medium sauté pan with a tablespoon of canola oil until the oil is hot. Place 2 pieces of puff pastry in the sauté pan and cook until golden brown on one side. Flip over and begin to cook the other side, pressing the dough down with a spatula to compress the puff. When golden brown on both sides, remove the puffs and drain on paper towels.

Sprinkle with the coarse salt and thyme. Serve warm or cold.

Makes 12 flatbreads.

SALMON RILLETTES

This is a nice pantry item to keep on hand for entertaining. We use it as a lodge appetizer as well as in our picnic baskets.

1 SMALL FILLET RED SALMON, BONED AND SKINNED

5 TABLESPOONS UNSALTED BUTTER

1 TABLESPOON PURE OLIVE OIL

1½ TABLESPOONS LEMON JUICE

½ SHALLOT, MINCED FINELY

1 TABLESPOON CHOPPED FLAT-LEAF PARSLEY

2 TEASPOONS CHOPPED TARRAGON

2 TABLESPOONS CHOPPED CHIVES

½ POUND HOT-SMOKED (KIPPERED) SALMON, FLAKED

SALT AND FRESHLY GROUND BLACK PEPPER

2 TABLESPOONS UNSALTED BUTTER, MELTED

1 SMALL FRENCH BAGUETTE, SLICED AND TOASTED

Rinse the fish and pat dry.

Fill a medium saucepan with enough water to come up about 2 inches. You can add aromatics such as herbs or wine to the water if you desire. Bring the liquid up to a boil then reduce it to a simmer. Poach the salmon in the liquid until fully cooked 5 to 7 minutes. Remove from the liquid and set aside.

In a medium mixing bowl, stir together the butter and the oil until smooth. Stir in the lemon juice, shallot, parsley, tarragon, and chives. Add in the smoked salmon.

Flake the poached salmon over the mixture, and then fold the pieces of salmon into the rillette mixture along with a pinch of salt and pepper.

Scoop the mixture into 3 half-pint glass canning jars or other serving containers and pour a medium thick layer of the melted butter over the rillettes creating a sealed cap. You may place herbs on top as a decorative touch. Chill the rillettes for at least an hour. Return to room temperature before serving. Serve with French bread toast points.

Makes 3 half-pints rillettes.

SEA CRACKERS

We make a kind of pastry from ground brown rice, add in our own seaweed, spices, and salt for an interesting appetizer cracker. We always enjoy new ways of highlighting uses of seaweed. You can use sheets or crumbles of nori available in the market.

1 CUP COOKED SHORT-GRAIN
  BROWN RICE

½ CUP ALL-PURPOSE FLOUR

6 TABLESPOONS WARM WATER

3 TEASPOONS SOY SAUCE

4 TABLESPOONS DRIED SEAWEED,
  DIVIDED

1 TABLESPOON BLACK SESAME SEEDS

1 TEASPOON BAKING POWDER

½ TEASPOON BAKING SODA

1 TABLESPOON COARSE SEA SALT

Preheat the oven to 300°F. Grease two sheets of parchment paper.

Place the brown rice into a food processor fitted with the metal blade and pulse until the rice forms a loose dough.

Add in the flour, water, soy sauce, 3 tablespoons of the seaweed, sesame seeds, baking powder, and baking soda into the food processor and pulse to combine all the ingredients into a cohesive dough.

Roll out the dough between the sheets of greased parchment paper. Roll the dough to ¼-inch thickness. Peel the top parchment off of the cracker. Place the dough in the center rack of the oven.

Bake the cracker dough for about 40 minutes until it is crisp and golden. Remove the cracker from the oven, cool slightly, and break the crackers into individual shards.

Sprinkle the crackers with the remaining seaweed and coarse salt.

Makes about 16 servings.

AT THE TABLE WE SHARE OUR STORIES

TO THE TABLE

Shopping for food we put onto the dinner table at the lodge often involves adventure.

If we go out my front door and walk across the deck, slide down the steel ramp, and climb onto the boat tied up to the end of the dock—and then head south into the deep and beautiful seven-mile fjord called Tutka Bay—we can go shopping for Alaska tanner crab.

The currency for obtaining crab in Tutka Bay is a few old pieces of salmon or halibut pinned to the inside of a square wire crab pot. In the short version, I drop the baited pot down into the deepest part of the bay. The pot is attached to a rope with a buoy on the end of it that bobs and floats to let me know where my crab pot is. In about twenty-four hours, I pull up the pot using a mechanized wench attached to the boat and count the number of trapped crabs I have.

It's a little bit like gambling. And that's why it's kind of addictive—I don't know what's coming up and I can't buy the pot.

When I go out to check for crabs, I wear bright orange rain bibs I bought at the marine hardware store over in Homer along with my knee-high rubber boots. Overkill I know, but I like dressing the part. My only problem—and it's a crazy one for a chef, which I am—is that I don't like to kill living things.

One recent summer, when I pulled up my crab pot, there was a giant octopus draped around the pot.

I screamed; he glanced up at me, stared me directly in the eye, and then gracefully uncoiled himself from the pot and slid back down into the depths. At the time I had a Spanish chef working at the lodge. He couldn't believe I let the octopus go.

"In Bilbao, I take them and I smash them in the head until they die," he told me with wild hand gestures and a fiery glint in his eye.

So I think about the crab, lured by a few pieces of old fish and now trapped in the pot, and if that isn't the least of its worries, there's a giant octopus trying to reach in and grab a leg or two. It's a brutal world. I've been known to let live crabs go on our beach and watch them return into the water. I am possibly the only catch-and-release

There are so many kinds of boats in the Homer harbor; the scene is a pleasant mix of small and large, pleasure craft and working boats.

The Homer Spit is home to a festive and slightly gaudy row of mostly sea-themed shops that hawk wares to tourists in the summer. (This includes our own small gift shop, the Rustic Wild.) You can find anything from buckets of crabs for sale to sweaters knitted in the Andes. Our little five-table café, La Baleine, serves organic cuisine, for breakfast and lunch only. The Spit boards up promptly on Labor Day with only a few spots remaining on for local winter trade.

Homer is the kind of town where a Canada goose makes headline news in the local paper. One year, a goose imprinted onto a group of sandhill cranes as a youngster. The entire town was riveted on the fate of the goose.

It's also the kind of town that has an annual ceremony on the beach where a big handwoven, two-story basket is built and then burned down, a transient piece of art used in a cleansing and healing ceremony of sorts. There are often fire dancers and drummers and a potluck on the beach. It is right up my alley.

"I hope they don't dump all that debris in the ocean," my husband, Carl, said when he first witnessed the event. He's a little more pragmatic about cleansing and healing ceremonies.

We buy rockfish and halibut for the lodge from a quaint wholesale fish market a few doors down from the café. Sometimes we wait for a boat to come in, delayed by tide or sea, and there we are, on the docks, waiting for our fish as the

crab fisherman in Alaska. Needless to say, it's easier for me to call my fish broker and order a fifty-pound case of crab legs delivered.

It takes twenty-five minutes from Tutka Bay to boat over to Homer, the seaside village where the endlessly fascinating marine hardware store is. I have a small apartment along the Homer harbor, on the Spit, as the peninsula that juts out from the mainland is called. I stay on the Homer side sometimes when I am transitioning between our two lodges and when I want to spend time at our little café nearby. My second-story, one-room apartment sits across from the public dock where huge boats pull in at all hours of the night, off-loading halibut, rockfish, and black cod. The fish are disgorged from the boats onto the dock; they are put straightaway into large, ice-filled totes and shipped off to fish markets around the world. The whole process takes minutes.

boat arrives. It is whisked away onto our boat, the *Sea Salt*, and ferried across the bay back to the lodge.

We buy from commercial fishermen who pull right up to our dock at the lodge bright chrome salmon, caught only minutes before. We haul large king salmon up to the kitchen in our garden cart. There is plenty of interesting conversation in our kitchen about exactly when to fillet a fresh salmon—after rigor mortis is completed, or before it sets in too vigorously, a window of only a few hours after the fish is caught. If we prepare a pre-rigor salmon, I usually trim out the fish bones from the flesh with a small knife rather

than try to pull them away with my Japanese fish tweezers. They won't pull out prior to rigor and attempting to do this rips the flesh.

I purchase scallops and shrimp from a fishmonger in Anchorage who has access to the best seafood all over Alaska. He will drive an order over to the Ted Stevens International Airport and send it to Homer on a small jet commuter flight. An employee will pick up the freight at the airport and get it onto a boat to the lodge. All can happen within the window of a couple hours.

When we go shopping for oysters, we bring out the kayaks, slip into the water, and head toward Seldovia and Jakolof Bay. Friends Frank and Margo Reveil operate the Jakolof Bay Oyster Farm, a fantasy landscape of silently floating lantern nets suspended in the cold Kachemak Bay. The multilevel mesh lanterns where the oysters live are kept in place by brightly colored floats lined up in neat rows along the bay. The scene looks futuristic and ancient all in the same moment.

Oysters aren't indigenous to Alaska. Farmers like the Reveils purchase oyster seed from outside and allow them to thrive and grow slowly in their lanterns for three to five years before harvesting. In their last year, the oysters are laid out onto algae-rich flats where tidal flux washes over and strengthens them. Many, including me, consider Kachemak Bay oysters to be the best in the world.

And, on it goes. Everything that is served on the Tutka Bay Lodge dinner table has a story.

BEEF FILET WITH JAKOLOF BAY OYSTER SAUCE

We are lucky to live near an oyster farm, close enough for us to kayak to. We take guests to visit the farm, purchase oysters, and head back to the lodge to cook them. I like this dish. The oysters complement and enrich a potentially boring cut of beef. If you don't have mushroom stock, use the soaking liquid from reconstituting dehydrated mushrooms.

3 TABLESPOONS CLARIFIED BUTTER (SEE PAGE 208)

1 POUND FRESH WILD MUSHROOMS, TORN INTO BITE-SIZED PIECES

2 TABLESPOONS CANOLA OIL

SALT AND FRESHLY GROUND BLACK PEPPER

4 FILETS BEEF TENDERLOIN (4 TO 6 OUNCES EACH)

12 JAKOLOF BAY OYSTERS, WASHED, SHUCKED, AND LIQUEUR REMOVED AND RESERVED

¼ CUP STORE-BOUGHT OR HOMEMADE QUICK BEEF STOCK (SEE PAGE 60)

3 TABLESPOONS OYSTER SAUCE

1½ CUPS HEAVY WHIPPING CREAM

1 TEASPOON LEMON JUICE

2 TABLESPOONS MINCED GREEN ONIONS

Preheat the oven to 400°F. Line a 13-by-18-inch baking sheet with parchment paper.

In a medium sauté pan over medium heat, melt the clarified butter. Add in the mushrooms and sauté until they have released and reabsorbed their liquid, about 10 minutes. Set aside.

Heat another large sauté pan over high heat. Pour in the canola oil and heat until very hot. Salt and pepper the beef filets. Place the filets in the hot oiled pan and sear them on both sides, about 3 to 4 minutes per side. Transfer the beef to a baking pan and place in the oven for about 5 minutes.

While the beef is cooking, make the sauce. Transfer the mushrooms to the sauté pan used to cook the beef. Set the pan over medium-high heat and pour in the reserved oyster liqueur, beef stock, and oyster sauce, bringing to a simmer. Stir in the cream and reduce about 4 minutes. Add in the oysters and cook until plumped. Stir the lemon juice into the sauce and add the green onions.

Serve the filets garnished with the mushroom-oyster sauce.

Makes 4 servings.

BRAISED SHORT RIB RAVIOLI

This is a nice first or main course dish that is easy to prepare once you get the hang of making the ravioli. We sometimes serve this with moose meat in the winter. Our inspiration for this came from spending time in Italy learning how to make pasta with two old ladies who ran a tiny restaurant in the Lakes region.

For the Braised Short Rib

1 POUND BEEF SHORT RIB

SALT AND FRESHLY GROUND BLACK PEPPER

2 TABLESPOONS EXTRA-VIRGIN OLIVE OIL

1 YELLOW ONION, PEELED, QUARTERED, AND SLICED

1 CARROT, PEELED AND CHOPPED

1 CELERY RIB, CHOPPED

2 CLOVES GARLIC, PEELED AND MINCED

2 CUPS STORE-BOUGHT OR HOMEMADE QUICK BEEF STOCK (SEE PAGE 60)

1 CUP APPLE CIDER

For the Filling

1 TABLESPOON PURE OLIVE OIL

1 YELLOW ONION, PEELED AND SLICED

½ CUP DOMESTIC MUSHROOMS, TRIMMED AND SLICED

SALT AND FRESHLY GROUND BLACK PEPPER

1 POUND BRAISED SHORT RIB, SHREDDED

½ CUP SHREDDED PARMIGIANO-REGGIANO CHEESE

2 TABLESPOONS MINCED CHIVES

1 LARGE EGG YOLK

TO MAKE THE SHORT RIB: Trim the meat of any fat or sinew. Wash the meat and pat dry. Salt and pepper it well. Heat the oil in a high-sided pan or stockpot. Sear the meat on both sides in the hot oil. Remove the meat and set aside.

Using the same pan, sauté the onion, carrot, celery, and garlic over medium heat for about 5 minutes. Add the short rib to the vegetable mixture. Cover the mixture with the beef stock and apple cider. (If the liquid doesn't completely cover the vegetables and meat, add more stock, cider, or water.) Cover the pan with a lid and simmer over low heat for 2 to 3 hours or until the meat is tender. Remove the meat and discard the liquid and vegetables. When cooled, shred the meat with two forks. Set aside.

TO MAKE THE FILLING: Place 1 tablespoon of olive oil in a sauté pan. Add in the onion and sauté over low heat for about 20 minutes or until the onions are lightly browned and completely softened. Add in the mushrooms and cook over low heat until the mushrooms are soft. Season with the salt and pepper to taste. Cool completely.

In a medium mixing bowl, combine the shredded Braised Short Rib meat, the onions and mushrooms, cheese, chives, and egg yolk. Salt and pepper to taste.

Makes about 2½ cups filling.

TO ASSEMBLE THE RAVIOLI: Line a 13-by-18-inch baking sheet with cornmeal.

Roll the pasta dough out on a floured work surface to ⅛-inch thickness. Cut the dough into 4 long strips, about 12 inches long and at least 3 inches wide.

For Assembly

CORNMEAL FOR DUSTING

1 POUND PASTA DOUGH
  (SEE PAGE 214)

SALT

Place a tablespoon of the filling along one strip of pasta at about 4-inch intervals. Cover with another strip of pasta to form the top. With moistened fingers, lightly press the two pasta strips together with your fingers around the mounds of the filling.

Use a 2-to-3-inch round or square ravioli cutter to cut out the ravioli. Place the ravioli onto the prepared baking sheet so they don't stick. Gather the scraps of dough and knead to create additional pasta strips if necessary.

If you are cooking the ravioli immediately, drop them into just-simmering salted water. They will take only 3 to 4 minutes to cook, rising to the surface. Toss the ravioli in a favored sauce or in olive oil and grated cheese. If you are serving the ravioli later, freeze them in an airtight container.

Makes about 24 (3-inch) raviolis.

MIXED HERB SALAD WITH PICKLED RADISH

We make this salad in some variation almost every day throughout the summer.

For the Vinaigrette

1½ TABLESPOONS APPLE CIDER VINEGAR

1½ TEASPOONS FINELY GRATED LEMON ZEST

3 TABLESPOONS LEMON JUICE

2 TABLESPOONS MINCED SHALLOTS

3 TABLESPOONS EXTRA-VIRGIN OLIVE OIL

For the Pickled Radish

4 SMALL RADISHES, SLICED

½ RED ONION, PEELED AND SLICED

2 CUPS RED WINE VINEGAR

½ CUP GRANULATED SUGAR

For the Mixed Herb Salad

6 CUPS MIXED GREENS FROM THE GARDEN, WASHED

¼ CUP TARRAGON LEAVES

¼ CUP FLAT-LEAF PARSLEY LEAVES

¼ CUP MINT LEAVES

¼ CUP MINCED CHIVES

¼ CUP CILANTRO, STEMMED

10 PICKED FIREWEED FLOWERS (OPTIONAL)

TO MAKE THE VINAIGRETTE: Combine the apple cider vinegar, lemon zest, lemon juice, and shallots in a small mixing bowl. Whisk in the olive oil to emulsify.

TO MAKE THE PICKLED RADISH: Combine the radishes and red onion in a small heatproof bowl.

In a medium saucepan over high heat, bring the red wine vinegar and sugar to a boil. Pour the hot mixture over the radishes and red onion. Cover and let sit for 1 hour at room temperature.

TO MAKE THE SALAD: In a large mixing bowl, toss the greens with the tarragon, parsley, mint, chives, and cilantro.

Pour two-thirds of the vinaigrette in the bottom of a large serving bowl. Add in the mixed greens. Toss with your hands or utensils to mix. Season with salt and pepper and toss again. Drizzle the remaining vinaigrette over the top of the greens. Transfer the salad to plates. Place the pickled radish and onion around the salad greens. Garnish with fireweed petals.

Makes 4 servings.

HALIBUT WITH RHUBARB AND GINGER

Rhubarb makes almost any dish more colorful and we especially appreciate it with halibut. Rhubarb and ginger complement each other and we use this combination in both savory and sweet dishes.

4 TABLESPOONS CANOLA OIL, DIVIDED

2 CLOVES GARLIC, MINCED

2 TABLESPOONS MINCED GINGER

1 CUP THINLY SLICED RHUBARB, TOSSED WITH 1 TEASPOON GRANULATED SUGAR

3 GREEN ONIONS SLICED THINLY

2 TABLESPOONS RICE VINEGAR

2 TABLESPOONS SOY SAUCE

2 TABLESPOONS HONEY

SALT AND FRESHLY GROUND BLACK PEPPER

2 HALIBUT FILLETS, (6-OUNCES EACH), RINSED AND PATTED DRY

Heat the oven to 350°F.

Heat 2 tablespoons of the oil in a heavy sauté pan over medium high heat. Add the garlic and ginger and cook for about 30 seconds. Add in the rhubarb and stir-fry for an additional 30 seconds. Add in the green onions, vinegar, soy sauce, and honey. Cook to heat through. Season with salt and pepper to taste.

Heat the remaining 2 tablespoons of canola oil in a medium nonstick sauté pan on high heat. Season the halibut with salt and pepper and add the fillets presentation-side down into the sauté pan. Sear on one side and place in the oven for about 2 to 3 minutes, depending on the thickness of the fish.

Serve the halibut, presentation-side up and drizzled with the sauce.

Makes 2 servings.

DARK CHOCOLATE BLACKBERRY TART

When we photographed this recipe, the entire office ate it immediately after the photo was taken. It can be dressed up with different fruits and garnish. We like to combine dried and fresh fruits together.

For the Crust

½ CUP (1 STICK) UNSALTED BUTTER, CHILLED AND CUT INTO 8 PIECES

¼ CUP GRANULATED SUGAR

1 LARGE EGG YOLK

1¼ CUPS ALL-PURPOSE FLOUR

¼ TEASPOON SALT

For the Chocolate Filling

12 OUNCES DARK CHOCOLATE 70 PERCENT COCOA, CHOPPED (ABOUT 2 CUPS)

1 CUP HEAVY CREAM

2 TABLESPOONS GRANULATED SUGAR

¼ TEASPOON SALT

½ CUP (1 STICK) UNSALTED BUTTER, ROOM TEMPERATURE

2 EGG YOLKS

½ CUP SOUR CREAM

For Assembly

4 TABLESPOONS BLACKBERRY JAM

1 PINT (2 CUPS) RIPE BLACKBERRIES, GENTLY RINSED AND LAID OUT ON A TOWEL TO DRY

½ CUP DEHYDRATED BLACK-BERRIES

TO MAKE THE CRUST: Preheat the oven to 350°F.

Pulse the butter and sugar in a food processor fitted with a metal blade until combined. Add the egg yolk and pulse a few times more. Add the flour and salt and process just until the dough holds together when you press it between your fingers.

Knead the dough briefly to bring all the ingredients together, then press it into a flat disk about 6 inches in diameter, wrap in plastic, and refrigerate until firm, about 30 minutes.

Roll the dough out onto a lightly floured work surface to ⅛-inch thickness. Roll the dough circle up onto the rolling pin and unroll it over an ungreased 10-inch tart pan with a removable bottom, centering the dough and pressing it firmly into the bottom and sides of the pan. Trim the top by rolling a rolling pin over the edges.

Bake the tart shell on the middle rack of the oven until the crust is light golden brown, 20 minutes. Set the pan on a rack to cool.

TO MAKE THE FILLING: Place the chocolate into a medium mixing bowl.

Bring the cream, sugar, and salt to a full, rolling boil in a medium saucepan.

Pour the boiling cream over the chocolate and let it sit a few seconds to begin melting, then stir gently with a whisk just until the chocolate is smooth.

Whisk in the butter, about a tablespoon or two at a time, until each piece is incorporated. Whisk in the egg yolks until smooth. Fold in the sour cream.

TO ASSEMBLE: Spread the jam onto the bottom of the tart shell evenly. Pour the chocolate filling into the tart shell and top with both fresh and dehydrated berries. Set the tart aside at room temperature, uncovered, until it is completely cooled and softly set, about 1 hour.

Makes 1 (10-inch) tart.

CARAMEL NUT TART

This recipe makes 2 tarts—one to eat now, one to save for later. Or, you can use small individual tart pans as we often do and make enough for a dinner party.

3½ CUPS CHOPPED NUTS, DIVIDED

2 CUPS ALL-PURPOSE FLOUR

⅔ CUP POWDERED SUGAR

1½ CUPS UNSALTED BUTTER, DIVIDED

½ CUP PACKED BROWN SUGAR

½ CUP HONEY

3 TABLESPOONS HEAVY CREAM

Preheat the oven to 350°F. Grease two 9-by-1-inch fluted tart pans with removable bottoms.

In a food processor, combine 1 cup of the nuts, the flour, powdered sugar, and ¾ cup of the butter, pulsing until the mixture is finely ground.

Use your hands to press the mixture into both tart pans to form the crusts. Bake the tart shells for 7 to 10 minutes or until the shells are golden around the edges.

While the tarts are baking in the oven, combine the remaining 2½ cups of nuts, the remaining butter, brown sugar, honey, and heavy cream into a medium saucepan. Bring the mixture to a boil for 1 minute and then pour the hot mixture evenly into the 2 tart shells. Let the tarts set for about 2 hours until they are firm.

Makes 2 (9-inch) tarts.

ALMOND CHOCOLATE TOFFEE

These little treats are a fond childhood memory for me. My mother and I once took a long boat ride from San Francisco to Southeast Asia. Along the way, I purchased all the toffees from the ship's purser and they tasted exactly like these do.

½ CUP (1 STICK) UNSALTED
　BUTTER

¾ CUP PACKED BROWN SUGAR

1 TEASPOON HONEY

¼ TEASPOON SALT

2 CUPS TOASTED ALMONDS,
　CHOPPED, DIVIDED

8 OUNCES SEMISWEET
　CHOCOLATE

Prepare 2 mini-loaf pans (3½-by-7-inch) by lining them with greased aluminum foil.

In a medium saucepan over medium heat, melt the butter. Add in the brown sugar, honey, and salt. Stir until the mixture reaches 290°F. This will take about 5 to 6 minutes.

Remove the pan from the heat and stir in 1 cup of the nuts.

Place the remaining 1 cup of nuts into a small mixing bowl.

Pour, or more accurately scrape, the toffee into the prepared loaf pans.

Let the toffee cool for a couple of minutes, and then lift the aluminum foil and contents out of the pans. Peel the loosened toffee onto an oiled cutting surface. Slice the toffee into in ½-by-2-inch bars. Let the bars cool.

Melt the chocolate over a double boiler if you have one. If not, watch cautiously as the chocolate melts over low heat. Some people prefer to melt chocolate in a microwave but we don't have one and don't cook with this method. Dip each piece of toffee into the melted chocolate and then roll it in the bowl of chopped nuts. We use a fork to lift the rolled toffee out of the nuts and place each onto a baking sheet.

Refrigerate the toffees for about 30 minutes before serving, or until the chocolate is nice and firm. Wrap them individually and festively and give them away for good luck.

Makes about 24 toffees.

GRILLED RIBEYE WITH OCEAN-STYLE CHIMICHURRI SAUCE

We have a great source for locally raised beef. Ribeye is a popular cut we use often. We like to serve beef with mild ocean flavors to remind guests where they are.

For the Ribeye

1½ CUPS DRY SHERRY WINE

½ CUP SHERRY VINEGAR

1 CUP RED ONION, SLICED

2 TABLESPOONS MINCED GARLIC

½ CUP PURE OLIVE OIL

4 BEEF RIBEYE STEAKS,
   6 OUNCES EACH

SALT AND FRESHLY GROUND
   BLACK PEPPER

**For the Ocean-Style Chimichurri
   Sauce**

1 CUP EXTRA-VIRGIN OLIVE OIL

⅔ CUP SHERRY WINE VINEGAR

1 TABLESPOON HONEY

2 TABLESPOONS LEMON JUICE

1 CUP CHOPPED FLAT-LEAF PARSLEY

4 TABLESPOONS CHOPPED FRESH
   BASIL LEAVES

1 TABLESPOON CHOPPED FRESH
   OREGANO LEAVES

½ CUP CHOPPED DRY NORI SHEETS

3 TABLESPOONS MINCED GARLIC

2 TABLESPOONS MINCED
   SHALLOTS

SALT AND FRESHLY GROUND
   BLACK PEPPER

¼ TEASPOON CRUSHED
   RED PEPPER FLAKES

TO MAKE THE RIBEYE: In a shallow mixing bowl large enough to hold the steak, combine the wine, vinegar, red onion, garlic, and olive oil. Stir to blend well.

Lay the steak over the marinade and turn it over. Wrap loosely and refrigerate for 30 minutes, being sure to turn the steak over at least once.

Remove the steak from the marinade and season with the salt and pepper. Grill the steak over high heat for 4 to 5 minutes per side. Remove from the grill and let rest for 5 minutes before thinly slicing across the grain.

Serve the ribeye with our Ocean-Style Chimichurri Sauce drizzled over the steaks.

Makes 4 servings.

CHIMICHURRI SAUCE

This sauce also goes well with grilled vegetables and even grilled oysters.

TO MAKE THE SAUCE: In the bowl of a food processor, combine the olive oil, vinegar, honey, lemon juice, parsley, basil, oregano, nori, garlic, and shallots. Pulse until well blended but do not purée.

Add in salt and pepper to taste and the crushed red pepper flakes. Transfer the sauce to a small glass mixing bowl and cover with plastic wrap for at least 1 hour at room temperature.

Makes 2 cups sauce.

CARROT GINGER SOUP

We serve this soup year-round as we always have an abundance of freshly harvested or well-stored Alaska carrots on hand. We make our own root vegetable chips but you can purchase these readily in the market.

1 TABLESPOON CANOLA OIL

2 TEASPOONS HOMEMADE CURRY POWDER (SEE PAGE 213)

1 CLOVE GARLIC, MINCED

1 (1-INCH) KNOB OF GINGER, PEELED AND MINCED

½ MEDIUM YELLOW ONION, PEELED AND DICED

1 POUND CARROTS, PEELED AND SLICED INTO ¼-INCH ROUNDS

1 BAY LEAF

2½ CUPS STORE-BOUGHT OR HOME-MADE ONE-HOUR CHICKEN STOCK (SEE PAGE 60)

½ CUP CANNED COCONUT MILK, PLUS EXTRA FOR GARNISH

1 CUP CARROT OR OTHER ROOT VEGETABLE CHIPS

Heat the canola oil in a medium high-sided saucepan over medium heat. Add in the curry powder and "cook" the powder for about 30 seconds.

Add in the garlic and stir. Cook for a minute or two.

Add in the ginger, onion, carrots, bay leaf, and chicken stock. Bring the mixture to a boil. Reduce the heat to medium low and simmer until the carrots are tender, about 20 minutes. Discard the bay leaf.

Working in batches, purée the soup in a blender until it is smooth. Pour the soup into a clean pot and return it to the stove over medium heat.

Stir in the coconut milk.

Serve with a swirl of coconut milk and a small nest of carrot or root chips.

Makes 4 servings.

WILD BERRY CHOCOLATE SHORTCAKE

You could, of course, purchase good quality ice cream and cut this recipe in half but we enjoy our ice cream maker and we use it nearly every day. Homemade ice cream always has a more vibrant flavor. You can keep the shortcakes whole or crumble them as we did.

For the Ice Cream

3 CUPS MIXED BERRIES

JUICE OF ½ LEMON

¾ CUP GRANULATED SUGAR, DIVIDED

3 EGG YOLKS

1½ CUPS HEAVY CREAM, DIVIDED

½ TEASPOON PURE VANILLA EXTRACT

PINCH OF SALT

4 OUNCES BITTERSWEET CHOCOLATE, COARSELY CHOPPED

2 TABLESPOONS WATER

LINE A 13-BY-18-INCH BAKING SHEET WITH PARCHMENT

For the Shortcake

⅔ CUP WHIPPING CREAM

1 TEASPOON PURE VANILLA EXTRACT

½ TEASPOON INSTANT ESPRESSO POWDER DISSOLVED IN 1 TABLESPOON HOT WATER

1½ CUPS ALL-PURPOSE FLOUR (PLUS EXTRA FOR DUSTING)

½ CUP GRANULATED SUGAR (PLUS 3 TEASPOONS FOR SPRINKLES)

⅓ CUP UNSWEETENED COCOA POWDER

1 TABLESPOON BAKING POWDER

½ TEASPOON SALT

¼ CUP (½ STICK) UNSALTED BUTTER, CHILLED, CUT INTO ½-INCH PIECES

TO MAKE THE ICE CREAM: Warm the berries in a small saucepan until they begin to release their juices. Add in the lemon juice. Purée the berries in a food processor and then strain through a fine mesh strainer to remove any seeds. You should have about 1 cup of juice. Stir in ¼ cup sugar.

Set a fine mesh strainer over a medium heatproof bowl. Set aside.

Whisk the egg yolks together in a small mixing bowl. Set aside

In a medium saucepan, heat ¾ cup of the cream and the remaining ½ cup sugar over medium heat, stirring until the sugar is dissolved. Whisk a bit of the hot mixture into the egg yolks. Then, mix the warmed yolks back into the hot mixture in the pot. Cook over medium heat, stirring constantly with a wooden spoon until the custard thickens enough to coat the back of the spoon. Don't let it come to a boil. Strain through the fine mesh strainer.

When the custard has cooled slightly, add in the remaining ¾ cup heavy cream, the strained berry purée, vanilla, and salt. Cover the custard with plastic wrap and refrigerate until chilled, about 30 minutes.

Melt the chocolate and the water in a double boiler, stirring frequently. Pour the mixture onto the parchment-lined baking sheet and freeze. When chocolate is firm, chop it into chunks. Return to the freezer until needed.

Freeze the custard according to your ice cream maker's instructions. While the ice cream is still soft enough, remove the ice cream into a medium stainless steel bowl. Fold in the chocolate chunks. Set the prepared ice cream in the freezer and make the shortcakes.

Makes 1 quart ice cream.

TO MAKE THE SHORTCAKE: Preheat oven to 400°F. Line two 13-by-18-inch baking sheets with parchment paper.

¼ CUP DARK CHOCOLATE, MELTED AND COOLED TO ROOM TEMPERATURE

2 TABLESPOONS UNSALTED BUTTER, MELTED

For Assembly

1 CUP FRESH BERRIES

In a small mixing bowl, whisk together whipping cream, vanilla, and the dissolved espresso powder.

In the bowl of a food processor fitted with a metal blade, mix in the flour, ½ cup of the sugar, cocoa powder, baking powder, and the salt. Add in the chilled butter. Pulse several times until the mixture is pea-sized.

Add in the chocolate and the cream mixture to the dough and pulse until moist clumps form.

Turn the dough out onto a lightly floured cutting board and form into a ball. Roll out the dough into a 1-inch-thick rectangle. Using a 2-inch round cookie cutter, cut out the shortcakes.

Place the shortcakes onto the prepared baking sheet, about 3 inches apart. Brush the melted butter onto the shortcakes. Sprinkle each with some of the remaining sugar.

Bake the shortcakes until a toothpick inserted into the centers comes out clean, about 15 minutes. Let the shortcakes cool on the baking sheet.

TO ASSEMBLE: Crumble some of the shortcake onto 6 serving plates. Scoop some of the ice cream over the crumbles and sprinkle with fresh berries.

Makes 6 servings.

SALMON WITH MISO BUTTER PASTA

We most often serve this with grilled salmon but the miso butter is good with chicken and other types of fish as well.

1 POUND STORE-BOUGHT OR HOMEMADE PAPPARDELLE PASTA (SEE PAGE 214 FOR PASTA DOUGH RECIPE)

2 TABLESPOONS CANOLA OIL

1 POUND RED SALMON FILLET, SKINNED AND BONED

SALT AND FRESHLY GROUND BLACK PEPPER

3 TABLESPOONS UNSALTED BUTTER

½ CUP SLICED SHALLOTS

¼ CUP YELLOW MISO PASTE

1 BUNCH FRESH BASIL, TORN INTO BITE-SIZED PIECES

Preheat the oven to 350°F.

Cook the pasta in boiling salted water until just al dente. Drain and set aside, reserving 1 cup of the pasta water.

Heat the oil in a medium sauté pan over high heat. Slice the salmon into 4 servings. Pat the salmon dry completely with a kitchen towel. Season with salt and pepper to taste. Add the salmon pieces into the hot pan and sear until a crisp edge forms. Place the pan in the oven to finish.

In another medium sauté pan over medium heat, melt the butter. Add in the shallots and sauté until they are soft, about 2 minutes. Add in the miso paste and the reserved pasta water. Simmer to reduce, about 3 minutes.

To serve, toss the pasta in the sauce. Place some of the sauced pasta onto the center of a wide individual serving plate. Sprinkle some of the basil over the pasta. Place a piece of seared salmon on top. Repeat with the remaining dishes.

Makes 4 servings.

TOASTED BARLEY RISOTTO WITH COMTÉ CHEESE

Comté cheese is one of our favorite cheeses to cook with. It is always in our pantry. It melts easily and has the flavor of nutty brown butter.

1 MEDIUM CAULIFLOWER, CORED

4 TABLESPOONS EXTRA-VIRGIN OLIVE OIL, DIVIDED

SALT AND FRESHLY GROUND BLACK PEPPER

3½ CUPS STORE-BOUGHT OR HOME-MADE ONE-HOUR CHICKEN STOCK (SEE PAGE 60)

1½ CUPS WATER

4 TABLESPOONS UNSALTED BUTTER, DIVIDED

1 CUP PEARL BARLEY

½ YELLOW ONION, PEELED AND DICED

4 GARLIC CLOVES, PEELED AND THINLY SLICED

¼ CUP DRY WHITE WINE

½ CUP GRATED COMTÉ CHEESE

2 TABLESPOONS FINELY CHOPPED FLAT-LEAF PARSLEY

Preheat oven to 425°F. Line a 13-by-18-inch baking sheet with parchment paper.

Cut the cauliflower into ½-inch pieces and toss them with 2 tablespoons of the oil and season with salt and pepper. Spread the cauliflower out in one layer onto the baking sheet and roast for 15 minutes, stirring occasionally, until the cauliflower is tender and well browned. Set aside.

Heat the stock and water in a small saucepan over medium heat.

Melt 2 tablespoons of the butter in a large heavy saucepan over medium heat. Toast the barley in the butter stirring constantly, 5 to 10 minutes. Add in the onion and garlic and cook until translucent. Add in the wine and simmer, stirring until absorbed, about 1 minute. Add in ½ cup of hot stock and briskly simmer, stirring, until absorbed.

Continue simmering and adding in hot broth, about ½ cup at a time, stirring constantly and letting each addition be absorbed before adding the next, until barley is tender, about 30 minutes.

Stir in the cauliflower, cheese, the remaining 2 tablespoons of butter, and season with salt and pepper to taste. Stir in the parsley. Thin the barley with a little of the remaining stock if desired.

Makes 4 servings.

ROSE PANNA COTTA WITH STRAWBERRIES

Panna cotta is a classic restaurant dessert that Mandy prepared often when she was the pastry chef at Ad Hoc restaurant in Napa. This version celebrates all the wild roses that grow in our area.

For the Panna Cotta

1½ TEASPOONS POWDERED GELATIN

2 TABLESPOONS ROSEWATER

3 CUPS SOUR CREAM

½ CUP BUTTERMILK

1¼ TEASPOONS PURE VANILLA EXTRACT

⅔ CUP GRANULATED SUGAR

12 ROSE PETALS FOR GARNISH

For the Strawberries

3 CUPS SLICED STRAWBERRIES

2 TABLESPOONS GRANULATED SUGAR

1 TABLESPOON ORANGE ZEST

PINCH OF SALT

TO MAKE THE PANNA COTTA: In a small mixing bowl, pour the gelatin in an even layer and then add the rosewater. Give it a stir and let set for about 5 minutes.

In a medium mixing bowl, whisk together the sour cream, buttermilk, vanilla, and sugar until thoroughly combined.

Ladle ½ cup of the sour cream-buttermilk mixture into a small saucepan and heat over medium-low heat, stirring constantly, until just warmed.

Add the softened gelatin to the saucepan and whisk constantly until it is dissolved. Remove the pan from the heat and set aside to cool for 5 minutes. Strain through a fine mesh strainer into a bowl or pitcher and pour the panna cotta into 6 (4- to 5-ounce) ramekins or molds.

Cover with plastic wrap and refrigerate for at least 5 hours or up to 2 days.

TO MAKE THE STRAWBERRIES: Mix all the ingredients together and chill in the refrigerator until panna cottas are ready.

TO ASSEMBLE: We usually serve panna cotta right in the ramekins they are poured into but you can unmold them. Run the tip of a knife gently around the edge of each panna cotta. Fill a medium wide mixing bowl with hot water and dip each ramekin two-thirds of the way up, then immediately unmold onto a serving plate.

Top the panna cottas with the macerated strawberries and rose petals.

Makes 6 servings.

RASPBERRY SEMIFREDDO

Semifreddo is a good recipe to keep around, particularly if you don't have an ice cream maker. This recipe makes about 12 dessert servings.

4 CUPS FRESH RASPBERRIES

1 TABLESPOON GRANULATED SUGAR

1 CUP POWDERED SUGAR, DIVIDED

4 LARGE EGG WHITES

2 CUPS CHILLED HEAVY CREAM

1 TEASPOON FINELY GRATED LEMON PEEL

2 TEASPOONS VANILLA PASTE

6 EACH STORE-BOUGHT LADY-FINGERS OR OTHER COOKIES

Line a 9-by-5-inch loaf pan with two layers of plastic wrap, leaving a long overhang. Stick the pan into the freezer.

Heat 2 cups of the raspberries in a small pot over medium heat with the granulated sugar. Add in a quarter cup of water. Once the berries have cooked down, purée them in a blender. Strain into a medium bowl. Cover and chill.

Using an electric stand mixer fitted with the balloon whisk, whip the egg whites to soft peaks. Add in $1/4$ cup of the powdered sugar. Beat the egg-sugar mixture until it is stiff. In a separate bowl, whip the heavy cream and the remaining powdered sugar until soft peaks form. Fold in the lemon zest, vanilla, and 1 cup of the raspberries. Fold the cream mixture into the egg white mixture. Transfer half of the mixture to the prepared pan. Layer in the cookies and add in the remaining cup of raspberries. Spoon half of the chilled raspberry sauce over the cookies. Pour in the remaining mixture. Cover the loaf with the plastic wrap, then foil. Freeze at least 4 hours. Unwrap the semifreddo. Turn out onto a platter. Remove the pan and peel off the plastic. Slice and serve with the remaining raspberry sauce.

Makes 1 loaf.

RED BEET AND SWEET POTATO CRUMBLE

This is an elegant first course or side dish. We love the blending of beets and sweet potatoes together with blue cheese and walnuts.

3 RED BEETS

6 SWEET POTATOES

3 TABLESPOONS EXTRA-VIRGIN OLIVE OIL (ADDITIONAL FOR THE CRUMBLE IF NEEDED)

SALT AND FRESHLY GROUND BLACK PEPPER

For the Crumble Topping

2 CUPS ROLLED OATS

½ CUP (I STICK) UNSALTED BUTTER, SOFTENED

¼ CUP SHROPSHIRE (OR OTHER) BLUE CHEESE

I CLOVE GARLIC, PEELED AND MINCED

½ CUP WALNUTS, COARSELY CHOPPED

¼ CUP SOURDOUGH BREADCRUMBS

¼ CUP PUMPKIN SEEDS

Preheat the oven to 400°F. Line two 13-by-18-inch baking sheets with parchment.

Peel and slice the beets and sweet potatoes into ⅛-inch-thick slices. Line the beets and sweet potatoes onto separate baking sheets. Drizzle with the oil and season with salt and pepper to taste. Place the baking sheets into the oven at the same time. Depending on the thickness of the beets and sweet potatoes, they may roast at different times. In general, it will take 25 minutes for the beets to cook and about 5 minutes less for the sweet potatoes.

Layer a 9-inch baking dish (or individual cast-iron pans like we did in our photo) with the beets and sweet potato, ending with the sweet potato. Season with salt and pepper to taste.

TO MAKE THE CRUMBLE TOPPING: In a medium mixing bowl, combine the oats, butter, blue cheese, garlic, walnuts, breadcrumbs, and pumpkin seeds. Add a little olive oil if the mixture is too dry.

Sprinkle the crumble generously on top of the sweet potato and beets.

Bake for 30 to 35 minutes, until golden brown.

Makes 4 servings.

SALMON-FILLED GNOCCHI

We think the color is so beautiful in these little filled gnocchi. It makes a lovely summertime first-course or main course meal.

For the Salmon Filling

I POUND RED SALMON, BONED AND SKINNED

½ CUP STORE-BOUGHT OR FRESH RICOTTA CHEESE (SEE PAGE 212)

¼ CUP GRATED PARMESAN CHEESE

I TABLESPOON CHIVES

¼ CUP CHOPPED ONIONS

I CLOVE GARLIC, PEELED AND MINCED

SALT AND FRESHLY GROUND BLACK PEPPER

For the Gnocchi

4 LARGE RUSSET POTATOES

I LARGE EGG

I LARGE EGG YOLK

I TEASPOON SALT

SALT AND FRESHLY GROUND BLACK PEPPER

I½ CUPS ALL-PURPOSE FLOUR, DIVIDED

For Assembly

6 TABLESPOONS UNSALTED BUTTER

2 TABLESPOONS MINCED FRESH SAGE

½ CUP GRATED GRUYÈRE CHEESE

COARSE SEA SALT

WILD MUSHROOM SAUCE, OPTIONAL (SEE PAGE 189)

TO MAKE THE FILLING: In a food processor, combine the salmon, ricotta, Parmesan, chives, onions, and garlic and purée to a smooth consistency. Season the mixture with salt and pepper to taste. Place the filling into a resealable plastic bag and set aside in the refrigerator while making the gnocchi dough.

TO MAKE THE GNOCCHI: Preheat the oven to 400°F.

With a fork, poke a few holes in each potato and spread them onto a baking sheet. Bake until potatoes are cooked through and tender, about 1 hour.

As soon as the potatoes are cool enough to handle, scoop out the flesh and pass it through a potato ricer or a food mill fitted with a small hole insert. Spread the potatoes onto a clean, lightly floured surface.

Whisk together the whole egg, egg yolk, and salt and drizzle over the riced potatoes. Sprinkle ¾ to 1 cup of the flour over the eggs.

With a bench scraper or two knives, work the ingredients together, cutting into them and gathering them into a mass. Add flour as needed to reduce stickiness.

When the mixture holds together, knead briefly, continuing to flour the work surface to prevent sticking and adding flour if the dough is sticky. As soon as the dough is smooth and soft, stop kneading and shape it into a thick log.

Working with ¼ of the dough at a time, roll the dough into long ½- to ¾-inch-thick ropes. Flatten each rope with the palm of your hand to make a 12-by-½-inch rectangle.

TO ASSEMBLE: Lightly flour a 13-by-18-inch baking sheet.

Horizontally pipe the salmon mixture down one side of a rectangle. Fold the other side of the rectangle over the salmon spread and pinch to seal. Roll the rectangle back and forth a bit to re-create the shape of a rope, sealing the salmon inside. Cut the rectangle into 1-inch pieces. Form ridges on the gnocchi by rolling them over the back of a dinner fork. Transfer the gnocchi to the baking sheet while rolling out remaining dough. Repeat the process with the remaining 3 rectangles.

At this point, you may refrigerate the uncooked gnocchi for up to 2 hours or freeze them on the baking sheet and then transfer them into a covered container and store in the freezer for several weeks.

Boil a large pot of water, add a generous pinch of salt, and blanch the gnocchi in two batches until they float. With a slotted spoon or spider, remove the gnocchi and spread onto a baking sheet.

While the gnocchi are cooking, heat the butter in a sauté pan over medium-high heat. Once the butter is melted and beginning to bubble, add in the sage. Continue to cook until the solid particles in the butter have browned lightly and the sage is crisp. Add the cooked gnocchi, tossing to coat the pasta evenly with the butter sauce. Allow the gnocchi to brown slightly. Sprinkle the gnocchi with the cheese and sea salt. We often serve with our Wild Mushroom Sauce (see page 189). Serve immediately.

Makes 4 main-course servings.

WHITE CHOCOLATE BREAD PUDDING WITH SIMPLE CARAMEL SAUCE

Anyone who knows our cooking knows that we always have a bread pudding in the works. We add other seasonal fruit to this recipe, either in the pudding itself or macerated and poured over as garnish. We often make a simple caramel sauce to serve with this recipe.

For the White Chocolate Bread Pudding

I POUND DAY-OLD SOURDOUGH BREAD, CUT INTO CUBES

UNSALTED BUTTER, FOR BAKING DISH

I CUP GRANULATED SUGAR, DIVIDED

I TART GREEN APPLE (SUCH AS GRANNY SMITH), WASHED AND CORED

I TABLESPOON GRATED LEMON ZEST

JUICE OF I LEMON

I TEASPOON GROUND CINNAMON

½ TEASPOON FRESHLY GRATED NUTMEG

½ CUP GOLDEN RAISINS

2 CUPS WHOLE MILK

6 OUNCES WHITE CHOCOLATE, COARSELY CHOPPED

3 LARGE EGGS

TO MAKE THE BREAD PUDDING: Preheat the oven to 350°F.

Bake the bread cubes—if they are not day-old and already slightly stale—for about 10 minutes just until they are crisped but still slightly soft in the middle.

Butter a medium (2-quart) baking dish. Sprinkle the dish with a small amount of the sugar.

Dice the apple into ¼-inch cubes. In a medium mixing bowl, combine the apple, lemon zest, lemon juice, cinnamon, nutmeg, raisins, and ½ cup of the remaining sugar. Add the bread cubes, mix, and turn the mixture into the baking dish, spreading out all evenly in the dish.

In a medium saucepan, combine the remaining ½ cup sugar and milk; stir frequently over low heat. Remove the mixture from the heat just as the milk starts to steam but don't let it boil. Add in the chocolate and stir until the chocolate is melted. This should only take a minute or two.

Whisk the eggs in a medium mixing bowl. Slowly whisk the warm milk mixture into the eggs, being careful not to cook the eggs.

Pour the white chocolate custard over the apple-bread mixture in the baking dish, covering the bread completely. Arrange a few pieces of apple to stick out of the pudding for contrast.

Place the baking dish onto the middle rack of the oven and bake for about 35 minutes, or until set.

Makes 6 to 8 servings.

For the Simple Caramel Sauce

2 CUPS GRANULATED SUGAR

¾ CUP UNSALTED BUTTER, ROOM TEMPERATURE, CUT INTO PIECES

1 CUP HEAVY WHIPPING CREAM

1 TABLESPOON SALT

1 TEASPOON PURE VANILLA EXTRACT

SIMPLE CARAMEL SAUCE

We sometimes add orange zest or substitute honey for the sugar in this recipe. We prefer caramel to be somewhat golden rather than dark amber. The longer you cook the sugar, the different the end results taste and look.

TO MAKE THE SAUCE: Heat the sugar in a heavy-bottomed medium saucepan over medium heat until the sugar is golden amber in color and completely melted, about 5 minutes. Sugar caramelizes at 350°F if you wish to use a candy thermometer, but we usually just watch for the golden color. Whisk in the butter.

Whisk in the cream, salt, and the vanilla extract. Remove the saucepan from the heat to cool the mixture for a few minutes.

Pour the cooled caramel into a glass jar for storage and cover the jar with a lid.

Caramel will last for up to 2 weeks in the refrigerator. Gently reheat before using.

Makes 2 cups sauce.

WEATHERVANE SCALLOPS WITH WHITE WINE SAUCE

Scallops are abundant during any time of the year except April and May. Sometimes we can buy them right off of boats anchored in the Homer harbor.

For the Scallops

12 WEATHERVANE SCALLOPS

SALT AND FRESHLY GROUND BLACK PEPPER

1 TABLESPOON CANOLA OIL

2 TABLESPOONS UNSALTED BUTTER

For the White Wine Sauce

2 TABLESPOONS UNSALTED BUTTER

4 CLOVES GARLIC, VERY FINELY CHOPPED

½ CUP WHITE WINE

JUICE OF ½ LEMON

4 TABLESPOONS CREAM

4 TABLESPOONS STORE-BOUGHT OR HOMEMADE QUICK BEEF STOCK (SEE PAGE 60)

SALT AND FRESHLY GROUND BLACK PEPPER

TO MAKE THE SCALLOPS: Pat the scallops very dry with a kitchen towel or paper towel. Season the scallops with salt and pepper to taste. Heat the canola oil and butter in a large sauté pan over medium-high heat. When the oil is hot, add in the scallops and cook for 5 minutes, turning them over halfway through.

TO MAKE THE SAUCE: Melt the butter in a medium saucepan and heat until foamy. Add in the garlic and sauté. Add in the wine and deglaze the pan. Cook for an additional 30 seconds, then stir in the lemon juice. Stir in the cream and stock. Simmer the sauce until it has reduced by half. Season with salt and pepper to taste.

TO SERVE: Drizzle a little of the sauce onto each plate. Top with 3 scallops, then drizzle with a bit more sauce.

Makes 4 servings.

PORK TENDERLOIN WITH LEEK CREAM

There are several pork growers locally in Alaska that produce very fine meat. Many farmers are raising their pigs organically and high-quality pork is always available to us.

For the Pork Tenderloin

1 (3-POUND) PORK LOIN ROAST, BONELESS

SALT AND FRESHLY GROUND BLACK PEPPER

¼ CUP CANOLA OIL

2 TEASPOONS DRIED BASIL

2 TEASPOONS DRIED ROSEMARY

2 TEASPOONS DRIED THYME

1 TEASPOON MINCED GARLIC

1 TABLESPOON BROWN SUGAR

¼ CUP DRIED APRICOTS

¼ POUND PISTACHIOS, SHELLED

LEEK CREAM

For the Leek Cream

2 CUPS HEAVY CREAM

4 SMALL LEEKS, WHITE AND LIGHT GREEN PARTS ONLY, CUT IN HALF LENGTHWISE AND WASHED

2 SPRIGS FRESH THYME

SALT AND FRESHLY GROUND BLACK PEPPER

TO MAKE THE PORK: Preheat the oven to 350°F.

Pat the pork loin completely dry with paper towel. Rub the loin well with salt and pepper.

Combine the oil, basil, rosemary, thyme, and garlic into a food processor fitted with a metal cutting blade. Pulse one or two times to combine. Add in the brown sugar and pulse until a paste is formed. Coat the loin completely with the paste. Cover and refrigerate overnight.

In a clean bowl of the food processor fitted with a metal cutting blade, chop the pistachios and apricots together until the consistency is quite fine and even. Coat the pork loin with the fruit-nut mixture.

Place the roast in a shallow pan. Cover the pork with foil and roast for 45 minutes.

Remove the foil and cook for an additional 20 minutes more to brown and crisp the outside. If you have an internal thermometer, it should read 145°F.

Serve with the Leek Cream.

Makes 4 to 6 servings.

LEEK CREAM

This is a nice sauce to accompany pork loin or any vegetable side dish.

TO MAKE THE CREAM: Bring the heavy cream to a boil then immediately reduce to a simmer in a medium saucepan. Add in the leeks and the thyme. Cook until tender, about 4 minutes. Remove the thyme stems.

Transfer the leek-cream mixture to a blender. Purée the leek mixture until smooth. Season with salt and pepper to taste. Serve warm.

Makes 1 cup leek cream.

OUR TEACHING LIVES

A GOOD COOK CAN COOK ANYWHERE

Mandy and I were in the Strait of Gibraltar heading toward Spain, sitting atop our twin beds in the stateroom of the cruise ship we were on. Papers were spread around us and we were crafting a quick plan to teach a last-minute add-on cooking class.

Outside our window, the Rock of Gibraltar rose behind giant waves splashing against the rails of the ship and we rocked back and forth as captain and crew navigated us through the storm. It was too violent to dock in Gibraltar as planned so Mandy and I, as the guest chefs onboard, were asked to throw together a little diversionary culinary entertainment as we made our way to Barcelona. We pulled it off, pots and pans rocking from side to side over the stovetop in the culinary theater and the crew teetering trays of samples through the crowd, as the ship tossed its way to the Mediterranean.

After our cooking class, we returned to our stateroom and peered into my laptop for news from home. Carl had sent an e-mail that our offer was accepted for a one-acre piece of property that sat adjoining the lodge. That was good news. The two properties were joined together by a little lagoon and we had hoped for privacy for our guests. The odd thing about the piece of land we just bought, however, was that the previous owners had dragged onto it an enormous old abandoned crabbing ship.

And, on the decking of this ship, they had built a two-story structure that can only be described as something of a Noah's Ark.

Almost immediately, we thought the crazy ship with two stories of wooden rooms could become a perfect cooking school. No running water, no ovens, no kitchen—no problem. The inherited kitchen at the lodge is a small galley-style space not suited for guests to gather round and join us.

As we sat on our beds in the storm, all the possibilities of the culinary world seemed to open up to us. What did we want to teach? What did we want to learn? We immediately went to work on how our newly acquired cooking school might take shape and form. We first outlined our own cuisine and what we had in our repertoire that we wanted to share with others.

Alaska cuisine, as we define it, is a blend of native culture and cuisine, a look to our pioneer heritage, Russian history, and shared geography of living along the north and west coasts of the Pacific Rim.

Native influence is found everywhere in our daily lives: how we care for and prepare our fish, in our art, clothing, and social life. I am always fascinated to learn old ways of food gathering, preparation, and preservation. A dish as simple as barbecued salmon over alder wood has a thousand-year legacy behind it.

we've adopted many cold-weather dishes. If you go to our annual state fair, you'll find jars of preserved red currants and plenty of baked goods in the Scandinavian style. We look to our northern neighbors for flavor, spices, and seasonally comforting dishes. You'll find cardamom in much of our repertoire, a northern influence rather than an Asian one.

And, now in the present day, Alaska's newer populations of Filipino, Korean, Hmong, African, and Pacific Islanders bring with them cuisines that inspire us. Kimchi is a common mainstay on the table and ethnic ingredients are found even in the smallest, far-flung Alaska markets.

Early Russian outposts brought cultivated gardens to Alaska. Russian settlers introduced beets, cabbage, and other hearty vegetables to the culinary landscape. You can find remnants of Russian cuisine sprinkled nearly everywhere in Alaska in dishes that have retained heritage or have morphed into modern versions. One example is coulibiac, or Russian salmon pie encased in pastry (there is a recipe for this dish in my *Winterlake Lodge Cookbook*). Coulibiac is as Alaskan a dish as it is Russian.

Pioneers in Alaska had it tough. Their contribution to our food culture still lingers in our can-do, hardworking Alaskan spirit. Our emphasis on canning and preserving, gardening and "putting food by" comes in part from those hard-living people. Sourdough, which is an essential in our kitchen, comes from this era.

We are geographically similar to Scandinavia, and through migration of fishermen and commerce,

Beyond our own foodways, Mandy and I wanted to learn about and tell the story of places we have visited and cuisines we admire. We knew we wanted to center our culinary collection within a manageable framework so we wouldn't be overwhelmed. We selected Japanese, Spanish, French, Indian, and Italian cuisines to focus upon for starters. Within each of those topics, we narrowed the scope a bit further.

In studying Japanese cuisine, we decided we wanted to be mentored by and study the cuisine of Elizabeth Andoh, the leading English-language expert on Japanese cookery. She is an award-winning cookbook author and teacher who lives in Tokyo. Later on, when we approached Elizabeth to ask if we might reference her books, she became a generous and available resource for us to learn from. Elizabeth and her husband came to visit us at Tutka Bay Lodge some time shortly after the 2011 Tōhoku earthquake. We were riveted by her stories of life in Japan during this terrifying and monumental time. Elizabeth's lyrical and poetic approach to Japanese food traditions is beautiful—both to read and to cook. In her stay with us, Elizabeth taught us treasured lessons, such as how to use a Japanese egg pan, how to make home-made dashi, and how to make our own sea broth.

Elizabeth Andoh emphasizes Washoku cuisine—a particular way of preparing Japanese ingredients and eating them in a codified traditional manner with particular utensils. Seasonal ingredients and dishes are paired with rice and miso soup. I've loved translating seasonality into my own cooking, such as dressing up a particular soup explicitly for winter or summer. Washoku cuisine, as defined by Andoh, is being mindful of:

- *Colors – balancing red, green, yellow, white, black*

- *Flavors – balancing sweet, salty, sour, bitter, spicy*

- *Methods – including boiled, seared, raw, fried, steamed foods*

- *Sourcing foods from both land and sea*

- *Sourcing foods locally, using seasonal, regional ingredients*

As we continued to craft our cooking school curriculum, we were now in Barcelona and immersed in Catalan cuisine. So, that was the second area of concentration we selected. Meandering through stalls of food at La Boqueria in Barcelona provided endless inspiration. Sitting atop two stools at the Pinotxo Bar, we sketched out what we admired most about coastal Catalan cooking. Spanish rustic sensibilities, use of fresh ingredients, and flavor-intensive palette is perfect for Alaska seafood. Using culinary author Colman Andrews as our literary guide and Catalan chef Carme Ruscalleda as inspiration, we worked our way through the countryside studying paellas, sauces, oils, and picada—an additive to sauces that contains in its simplest form nuts, bread, and some kind of liquid.

A picada recipe we reference in our kitchen involves pulverizing together a couple of cloves of garlic, a handful of roasted almonds, the same amount of roasted hazelnuts, a slice of fried bread, salt, and a small bunch of parsley sprigs. We cover the mash with some good quality Spanish olive oil. We most often add it to sauces or sometimes soups just moments before serving. It adds texture and flavor and it is completely addictive. A favorite Spanish culinary technique we share is how to peel a tomato on a box grater. Simply grate a whole unpeeled tomato through the large holes of the grater. The pulp goes through and the skin remains—an instantly peeled tomato.

When we thought about French cuisine, certainly we could have gravitated to our formal Cordon Bleu education but we were more inspired by reading through the new *Michelin Red Guide* we had in tow. In this French culinary roadmap, restaurants are rated from one star to three stars. Two stars represent "excellent cooking, worth a detour." Three stars mean "exceptional cooking—worth a journey." In our mind, two-star restaurants are much more interesting than the fine dining perfection those three stars represent. Many two-star restaurants are working hard toward their three-star status. So, we decided to study the cuisine of the slightly lesser star, in smaller villages or rural locales throughout France. It's been a unique way to explore the soul of French cooking, which we still believe to be the most passionate in the world.

It's from one of these small restaurants in the south of France where we learned to make our fisherman's stew. Certainly, a Provençal bouillabaisse (this word means boil then braise) might contain many sea creatures we don't find in Tutka Bay but the essence of our version is all France. In our recipe for Alaska Fisherman's Stew included in this collection, we often add rouille, a garlic-rich, red pepper deliciousness made by combining 1 roasted red bell pepper, 1 roasted red chile pepper, the juice of ½ lemon, 3 peeled garlic cloves, ½ cup of breadcrumbs, and ½ cup of parsley leaves. Purée all in a food processor. Drizzle good quality olive oil into the mixture until it makes a thick mayonnaise-like consistency.

We are in love with Indian cuisine and we study it sincerely. We made the decision to highlight West

India Goa Coast cuisine to complement our Alaska seafood but honestly, we enjoy it all. Goan cuisine is a fascinating amalgam of thousands of years of Muslim, Portuguese, and Hindu culinary history and tradition. It seems remarkable to me to make this ancient and complex culinary world come alive at moments in our wooden ship cooking school in Alaska.

One of the most fascinating techniques I have learned in Indian food cookery is how to handle spices. Each spice can be used whole or ground, raw or cooked, dry or in oil, and each of these combinations yields a slightly different version of itself. And, the spice combinations are nearly infinite. It is so much more fragrant and vibrant to dry-heat and grind your own spices.

We make our own version of Madras curry at the lodge and the recipe for it here is entitled Homemade Curry Powder (see page 213). Another staple favorite is garam masala, a kind of last-minute seasoning added into dishes. Our version of garam masala is dry-toasted chile, saffron, black peppercorns, whole cloves, cumin seeds, coriander seeds, fennel seeds, bay leaf, and ground nutmeg. (You can vary how much of each of these spices to use and accentuate the final product.) All is then ground up in the small coffee grinder we reserve for spices only. A fresh batch of garam masala might last only a few days depending on how it is stored. It should be kept in an airtight container away from light.

When we explored Italian cuisine possibilities, we disregarded our inclination to look toward heat and sun and we headed north. Northern Italian cuisine is, of course, a huge and complex topic, but we embrace it with such enthusiasm and excitement we know we will never tire of poking around Emilia-Romagna, Piemonte, Lombardy, and the Lakes Region. Gnocchi, ravioli, risotto, tiramisu, panna cotta, Robiola, Gorgonzola, Parmigiano-Reggiano, prosciutto, and porcini all find their way to our Alaska table. Italian cuisine enriches our lives and our indigenous foods. A delicious Northern Italian sauce we make frequently is bagna cauda, a garlicky, anchovy-oil sauce that we drizzle over seafood as well as serve more traditionally as a dip for bread and vegetables.

To make bagna cauda, take about a cup of good quality olive oil and heat it in a small saucepan. Add in 8 cloves of minced garlic, 8 chopped anchovy fillets, a little hot pepper sauce, a small handful of minced flat-leaf parsley, and salt and pepper.

By the time Mandy and I left our cruise-chef adventure and returned to the States, we had notebooks filled with recipes, ideas, and dreams. And, with the guidance of mentors and chefs, cuisines ancient and new, our cooking school has flourished. We still don't have a proper kitchen or running water or ovens yet, but we cook and teach and learn as we look out over the peaceful lagoon between the lodge and cooking school.

ALASKA FISHERMAN'S STEW

All summer long, we make this on the grill that is situated on the big deck right next to the ocean. We serve it rustic country style with big baskets of warm bread and carafes of wine. Serve this with our garlicky rouille sauce (see page 180).

2 TO 3 TABLESPOONS CANOLA OIL

2 SMALL RED POTATOES, CUT INTO EIGHTHS

1 MEDIUM CARROT, PEELED AND CHOPPED

½ RED ONION, PEELED AND CHOPPED

2 OUNCES SPANISH CHORIZO

3 GARLIC CLOVES, PEELED AND MINCED

3 ROMA TOMATOES, CHOPPED

1 CUP STORE-BOUGHT OR HOME-MADE ONE-HOUR CHICKEN STOCK (SEE PAGE 60)

½ CUP DRY WHITE WINE

½ TEASPOON SAFFRON THREADS, CRUSHED

¼ TEASPOON OREGANO

¼ TEASPOON CAYENNE PEPPER

8 LITTLENECK CLAMS, SCRUBBED

4 BUTTER CLAMS, SCRUBBED

8 MUSSELS, SCRUBBED AND DE-BEARDED

¼ POUND SPOT SHRIMP, PEELED

¼ POUND COD FILLET, SKINNED, BONED, AND CUT INTO 1-INCH PIECES

¼ POUND HALIBUT, SKINNED AND CUT INTO 1-INCH PIECES

¼ POUND SCALLOPS

1 TABLESPOON CHOPPED FRESH FLAT-LEAF PARSLEY

LEMON WEDGES, FOR GARNISH

SOURDOUGH BREAD

In a large saucepan over medium heat, heat 2 tablespoons of the canola oil. Add in the potatoes, carrots, onion, chorizo, and garlic. Sauté the mixture until the onion begins to soften, about 5 minutes.

Stir in the tomatoes, chicken stock, wine, saffron, oregano, and cayenne. Bring the mixture to a boil. Cover, reduce the heat, and simmer about 15 minutes.

Add in the littleneck clams, butter clams, and mussels and simmer, covered, an additional 3 minutes.

Discard any clams or mussels that don't open. Add the shrimp and cod and cook for an additional 5 minutes.

Heat a sauté pan to medium heat and add in a little canola oil. Season the halibut and scallops with salt and pepper to taste. Pan-sear them until they form a golden crust.

To serve, ladle some of the stew into a wide individual serving bowl. Add in pieces of the halibut and scallops onto the stew. Sprinkle with the parsley. Garnish with lemon wedges and serve with plenty of sourdough bread. Repeat with the remaining stew.

Makes 4 servings.

ALASKA SEAFOOD SAUSAGE

We use this sausage sometimes as a breakfast item but most often in savory bean dishes or stews. It also makes an appearance on barbecue days on the charcuterie board.

I POUND HALIBUT FILLET, SKINNED

½ POUND SCALLOPS

¼ POUND SPOT SHRIMP, PEELED

I TABLESPOON LEMON ZEST

½ SHALLOT, MINCED

I TEASPOON FINELY CHOPPED GARLIC

I TABLESPOON CHOPPED PARSLEY

½ TEASPOON FENNEL SEEDS

I PINCH PAPRIKA

2 LARGE EGG WHITES

SALT AND FRESHLY GROUND BLACK PEPPER

I TABLESPOON CANOLA OIL

Combine the halibut, scallops, shrimp, lemon zest, shallot, garlic, parsley, fennel seeds, paprika, and egg whites in a food processor using the metal blade attachment. Process until just combined. Season with salt and pepper to taste.

Lay out one 14-inch-long strip of plastic wrap. Spoon out one-third of the sausage mix lengthwise onto the film. Roll the sausage into a tight log about I inch thick. Tie the plastic wrap on each end of the log and twist it once in the middle. Repeat with two more 14-inch lengths of plastic wrap.

Fill a large high-sided sauté pan with water and bring to a boil, then reduce to a simmer. Submerge the wrapped sausages into the water and poach them until they are firm to the touch. Cool and unwrap.

Heat the canola oil in a medium sauté pan on high. Sear the sausages whole until they are browned on the outside. Slice and serve.

Makes 6 sausages.

CANDIED CRABAPPLES

You can make similar treats using regular small apples or even cherries. We used small twigs from a willow tree for this recipe but you can purchase sticks available at craft stores.

2 CUPS GRANULATED SUGAR

¼ CUP LIGHT CORN SYRUP

½ CUP WATER

½ CUP HEAVY CREAM

2 TABLESPOONS UNSALTED BUTTER

1 TEASPOON PURE VANILLA EXTRACT

¼ TEASPOON GROUND CINNAMON

⅛ TEASPOON SALT

½ CUP CHOPPED PECANS

½ CUP CHOPPED PISTACHIOS

12 TO 15 CRABAPPLES

MEDIUM-COARSE SALT

Line a 13-by-18-inch baking sheet with parchment. Grease the parchment.

Mix the sugar, corn syrup, and water in a small saucepan. Bring to a boil over medium-high heat, stirring just until the sugar dissolves. Cook over medium heat, swirling the pan (don't stir—that might cause crystallization), until the mixture is golden amber, about 8 to 10 minutes. Remove from the heat.

Slowly whisk in the heavy cream, unsalted butter, vanilla extract, cinnamon, and salt. Return to low heat and whisk until the mixture is smooth. Let the mixture cool until the caramel is thick enough to coat a spoon.

Place the pecans and pistachios into a medium mixing bowl. Insert small, sturdy sticks into the stem ends of the clean and dry crabapples. Dip the apples into the caramel, letting the excess drip off. Roll the apples in the nuts. Sprinkle with the salt. Let the apples cool on the prepared baking sheet.

Makes 12 to 15 candied crabapples.

FOUR SAUCES FOR SEAFOOD

Here are our suggestions for various sauces that work well with Alaska fish, particularly salmon.

Romesco Sauce

1 PASILLA CHILE PEPPER

3 ROMA TOMATOES, CORED
   AND HALVED LENGTHWISE

½ RED BELL PEPPER, CORED
   AND SEEDED

1 YELLOW ONION, HALVED

1 GARLIC CLOVE, PEELED AND SLICED

¼ CUP EXTRA-VIRGIN OLIVE OIL

SALT AND FRESHLY GROUND
   BLACK PEPPER

1 TABLESPOON CANOLA OIL

3 CRUSTLESS 2-INCH CUBES
   SOURDOUGH BREAD

10 TO 12 HAZELNUTS

1 TABLESPOON APPLE CIDER
   VINEGAR

½ TEASPOON SMOKED PAPRIKA

Savory Miso Sauce

5 TABLESPOONS RED MISO

1 TEASPOON POWDERED MUSTARD

3 TABLESPOONS GRANULATED SUGAR

2 TABLESPOONS DASHI

2 TABLESPOONS LEMON JUICE

2 TABLESPOONS SAKE

2 TABLESPOONS SOY SAUCE

2 TABLESPOONS LIGHT SESAME OIL

1 TABLESPOON GROUND TOASTED
   SESAME SEEDS

5 TABLESPOONS CANOLA OIL

Blueberry Demi-glace

1 SHALLOT SLICED

1 TABLESPOON UNSALTED BUTTER

ROMESCO SAUCE

Preheat oven to 400°F. Line a 13-by-18-inch baking sheet with parchment.

Remove the seed and stem from the pasilla chile. Put it into a small mixing bowl, cover with warm water, and soak for 30 minutes.

Put the tomatoes, bell pepper, onion, and garlic onto the baking sheet and toss with the olive oil, salt, and pepper. Roast the vegetable mixture for 30 minutes, until the vegetables are well browned. Remove the sheet from the oven and let cool slightly.

Remove the skins from the tomatoes and pepper. Discard the outer layer of the onion. Reserve any liquid in the pan.

Heat the canola oil in a small sauté pan over medium heat. Add in the bread and toast until browned on all sides. Remove the bread from the pan. Add in the nuts and toast until fragrant, about 30 seconds to 1 minute. Transfer to a plate.

Drain the pasilla chile. Put it into a blender with the tomatoes, bell pepper, onion, garlic, and any reserved liquid. Blend until smooth.

Add the apple cider and the paprika and blend until smooth. Season with salt and pepper to taste. Refrigerate covered for up to 2 weeks.

Makes 1 cup sauce.

SAVORY MISO SAUCE

In a medium mixing bowl, whisk together the miso, mustard, and sugar. Add in the dashi, lemon juice, and sake.

Pour the mixture into a small sauté pan and simmer over low heat to combine the flavors. Add in the soy sauce, sesame oil, and sesame seeds. Once the mixture has come to a simmer, pour the mixture back into the mixing bowl and drizzle in the canola oil while whisking to lightly emulsify. Keep warm.

Makes 1½ cups sauce.

½ CUP FRESH BLUEBERRIES

¼ CUP RED WINE

I CUP BEEF DEMI-GLACE

2 SPRIGS FRESH THYME

Wild Mushroom Sauce

2 TABLESPOONS PURE OLIVE OIL

2 SHALLOTS, PEELED AND MINCED

I CLOVE GARLIC, PEELED AND MINCED

2 CUPS WILD MUSHROOMS, CLEANED AND TORN INTO BITE-SIZED PIECES

SALT AND FRESHLY GROUND BLACK PEPPER

½ CUP WHITE WINE

3 TABLESPOONS UNSALTED BUTTER

4 TABLESPOONS ALL-PURPOSE FLOUR

I CUP WHOLE MILK

2 CUPS STORE-BOUGHT OR HOMEMADE QUICK BEEF STOCK (SEE PAGE 60)

I TABLESPOON SOY SAUCE

4 TEASPOONS CHOPPED FRESH DILL

2 TEASPOONS CHOPPED FRESH PARSLEY

I CUP SOUR CREAM

2 TEASPOONS PAPRIKA

BLUEBERRY DEMI-GLACE

In a medium sauté pan over medium high heat, sauté the shallots in butter until they are translucent. Add in the blueberries and deglaze the pan with the red wine. Simmer for about a minute. Add in the demi-glace and thyme and simmer an additional minute until the sauce coats the back of a spoon. Remove the thyme sprigs.

Makes 2 cups sauce.

WILD MUSHROOM SAUCE

Heat the oil in a large sauté pan over medium-high heat. Add the shallots and garlic to the pan. Add the mushrooms to the pan and season with salt and pepper to taste. Cook until mushrooms are tender and brown. Turn the heat to high. Add in the wine and deglaze the pan. Set aside.

In a medium saucepot with a lid, melt the butter and stir in the flour, constantly whisking for several minutes until the mixture is a rich, caramelized brown. Add the milk, stock, and soy sauce, still whisking until the mixture is smooth.

Add in the mushrooms, dill, and parsley. Bring to a boil, reduce the heat to medium, cover, and simmer for 15 minutes, stirring occasionally.

Stir in the sour cream, simmer for another 2 minutes. Add in the paprika. Season with salt and pepper to taste.

Makes 6 cups sauce.

MAKING SEA SALT

The name of our boat at the lodge is the Sea Salt. The men on our staff didn't really like the name at first but now they are used to it. We have toured several sea salt manufacturing sites around the world. Our efforts are more for fun than true production.

Gather seawater with a food-grade 5-gallon bucket. These are available at hardware stores. Pour the seawater into 9-by-13-inch glass baking pans or other shallow glass vessels. Cover the pans with thick cheesecloth and tape or band the edges to seal.

Place the pan in the sun to dehydrate. This can take a day or two depending on the weather. Strain the salt through a medium sieve to remove any bits of rock or seaweed.

In general, 5 gallons of seawater will produce slightly less than 1 pound of salt.

SALT-BAKED SALMON WITH LEMON AND FENNEL

This is an old-fashioned cooking technique that is still fun to do and present at the tableside.

1 WHOLE RED SALMON (AROUND 8 POUNDS)

2 LEMONS, THINLY SLICED

FRONDS FROM 1 FENNEL BULB

4 POUNDS COARSE SALT

Preheat the oven to 400°F.

Rinse the fish inside and out under cold running water, then pat it dry. Place the lemon slices and the fennel inside the cavity. Don't bother to season the fish.

Place the salt in a large mixing bowl and add enough cold water to yield the consistency of wet sand. (This can take as much as 4 cups, depending on the type of salt, but start with 1 cup of water.) Mix with your hands.

Spread half of the salt mixture onto a baking sheet large enough to hold the fish to create a flat, even surface. Lay the fish on top and cover with the rest of the salt, packing the salt firmly around the fish.

Bake the salmon for 15 to 20 minutes, or about 8 minutes per inch of fish. Set the baking sheet aside to rest and cool. The fish continues to cook in the salt until you crack it open. Serve the salmon tableside, cracking the salt crust open and discarding.

Makes 8 to 10 servings.

GOA-STYLE SHRIMP CURRY

We study the cuisine of the Goa Coast in our cooking school. I am fascinated by the region's history, food culture, and life lived near the sea.

I POUND ALASKA SIDESTRIPE SHRIMP

½ TEASPOON SALT

⅛ TEASPOON FRESHLY GROUND BLACK PEPPER

1½ TEASPOONS HOMEMADE CURRY POWDER (SEE PAGE 213), DIVIDED

4 TABLESPOONS CANOLA OIL, DIVIDED

I (I-INCH) KNOB GINGER, PEELED AND MINCED

I RED ONION, PEELED AND CHOPPED

2 GARLIC CLOVES, PEELED AND MINCED

½ TEASPOON TURMERIC

3 CUPS CANNED CHOPPED TOMATOES, WITH JUICE

2 CUPS COCONUT MILK

¼ CUP CHOPPED FRESH CILANTRO

4 CUPS COOKED BASMATI RICE

Place the shrimp into a medium mixing bowl and add in the salt, pepper, and I teaspoon of the curry powder. Mix well and set aside.

In a sauté pan over medium-high heat, combine 2 tablespoons of the canola oil, the ginger, and the onion. Sauté the mixture until the onion is soft and translucent. Add in the garlic and turmeric and sauté until fragrant, about I minute.

Reduce the heat to medium-low and add in the tomatoes. Stir for I minute, scraping the sides and bottom of the pan. Increase the heat to medium-high and simmer for 5 minutes, stirring often.

Stir in the remaining ½ teaspoon curry powder and cook for I minute. Add in the coconut milk and bring the mixture to a boil. Reduce the heat to a simmer.

While the curry is simmering, sauté the shrimp in the remaining 2 tablespoons of canola oil in a medium sauté pan over high heat. Cook until the shrimp are lightly colored. Add the shrimp into the curry. Stir in the cilantro. Serve over rice.

Makes 4 servings.

HALIBUT SHAWARMA

When Mandy lived in Pasadena, she loved to stop into a little Shawarma shop across the street from her culinary school. This food memory has created an Alaska version.

For the Marinade

1 CUP STORE-BOUGHT PLAIN YOGURT OR FRESH HONEY YOGURT (SEE PAGE 211)

2 CLOVES GARLIC, PEELED AND MINCED

2 CARDAMOM PODS

2 TEASPOONS HOMEMADE CURRY POWDER (SEE PAGE 213)

JUICE OF 1 LEMON

1 POUND HALIBUT FILLET, SKINNED AND DICED INTO 1-INCH CHUNKS

SALT AND FRESHLY GROUND BLACK PEPPER

For the Sauce

1 CUP STORE-BOUGHT PLAIN YOGURT OR FRESH HONEY YOGURT (SEE PAGE 211)

2 CLOVES GARLIC, PEELED AND MINCED

¼ CUP LEMON JUICE

1 CUCUMBER, SEEDED AND DICED

1 TABLESPOON APPLE CIDER VINEGAR

SALT AND FRESHLY GROUND BLACK PEPPER

For Assembly

2 TABLESPOONS CANOLA OIL

4 LARGE PITA ROUNDS

1 CUP CHOPPED ROMAINE LETTUCE

TO MAKE THE MARINADE: In a large mixing bowl, combine the yogurt, garlic, cardamom, curry powder, and lemon juice. Place the fish in the marinade, add salt and pepper to taste, and let it sit while you prepare the sauce.

TO MAKE THE SAUCE: Combine the yogurt, garlic, lemon juice, cucumber, and vinegar together in a small mixing bowl. Salt and pepper to taste. Set aside.

TO ASSEMBLE: Take the fish out of the marinade. Do not wipe the marinade off. Heat the canola oil in a medium sauté pan over medium-high heat and brown the halibut.

½ CUCUMBER, SLICED

½ CUP PICKLED RED ONION,
(SEE PAGE 215)

2 RED RADISHES, SLICED THINLY

1 ROMA TOMATO, SEEDED AND
DICED

½ CUP FRESH CILANTRO, PICKED

Place ½ cup of the fish into each pita and top with a sprinkle of lettuce, cucumber, pickled onion, radish, and tomato.

Drizzle some of the sauce over the fish, sprinkle with the cilantro, and wrap the pita tightly.

Makes 4 shawarma.

MARCONA ALMOND-CRUSTED HALIBUT CHEEKS WITH SIMMERED SOFRITO

One halibut cheek makes a nice first course serving. If you want to make this a main course dish, add more halibut. We've included another kind of sofrito with this recipe than the one we use for our paella. Marcona are specialty Spanish almonds readily available in the market.

For the Marcona Almond-Crusted Halibut

2 CUPS PANKO

1 TABLESPOON FRESH THYME

1 CUP CHOPPED MARCONA ALMONDS

1 LARGE EGG

1 CUP ALL-PURPOSE FLOUR

4 LARGE HALIBUT CHEEKS

SALT AND FRESHLY GROUND BLACK PEPPER

1 TABLESPOON UNSALTED BUTTER

COARSE SALT, TO FINISH

For the Simmered Sofrito

3 TABLESPOONS UNSALTED BUTTER

2 TEASPOONS CANOLA OIL

1 LARGE YELLOW ONION, PEELED AND CUT INTO ¼-INCH DICE

2 TABLESPOONS CHOPPED PANCETTA

SALT AND FRESHLY GROUND BLACK PEPPER

2 CARROTS, PEELED AND DICED

2 CELERY RIBS, DICED

3 CLOVES GARLIC, PEELED AND MINCED

2 RED BELL PEPPERS, SEEDED AND DICED

TO MAKE THE HALIBUT: Preheat the oven to 350°F.

Mix the panko, thyme, and almonds together in a medium mixing bowl. Whisk the egg in a separate medium mixing bowl. Place the flour in a third medium mixing bowl.

Dip each halibut cheek into the egg, then coat with flour. When all the pieces of halibut have been coated, dip in egg again before dipping into the almond panko mixture. Season with salt and pepper to taste.

Melt the butter in a medium sauté pan over medium heat. Add in the halibut cheeks and brown. Place the sauté pan in the oven for 2 to 3 minutes or until the cheeks are done. Sprinkle the breaded halibut cheeks with the coarse salt. Serve over the top of the sofrito.

Makes 4 first-course servings.

1 YELLOW BELL PEPPER, SEEDED AND DICED

6 LARGE ROMA TOMATOES

2 CUPS STORE-BOUGHT OR HOME-MADE ONE-HOUR CHICKEN STOCK (SEE PAGE 60)

1 BAY LEAF

1 SPRIG THYME

EXTRA-VIRGIN OLIVE OIL

TO MAKE THE SOFRITO: Heat the butter and canola oil in a medium high-sided saucepan over medium heat. Add in the onion and the pancetta and reduce the heat to low. Sauté the mixture until the onions are soft and translucent. Season with salt and pepper to taste. Add in the carrot, celery, garlic, and red and yellow bell peppers.

Grate the tomatoes on the large holes of a box grater. The pulp will go through the grater, creating a purée, while the skin remains in your hand. Discard the skins. Add this to the simmering sofrito.

Add in the stock, bay leaf, and thyme. Simmer on low until the carrots are cooked down and the ingredients have combined together. Drizzle in a little olive oil for flavor and texture. Add additional salt and pepper to taste if necessary.

Makes about 2 cups sofrito.

RAMEN NOODLE BOWL

To make a bowl of ramen, we heat the broth to piping hot. We place our tare (secret flavoring underneath the noodles) into the bottom of a deep-sided soup bowl. Next comes a nest of noodles, the hot broth, then vegetables, and Alaska salmon carefully placed on top. We often serve this with a poached egg.

For the Tare (secret flavoring)

1 TABLESPOON WHITE MISO

1 TEASPOON SAKE

For the Ramen Noodles

1 TABLESPOON BAKED BAKING SODA (BAKE SODA FOR 1 HOUR IN THE OVEN AT 300°F ON A SMALL ALUMINUM-LINED BAKING SHEET)

½ CUP WARM WATER

½ CUP COLD WATER

3 CUPS BREAD FLOUR

SALT

For the Broth

4 CLOVES

½ YELLOW ONION

2 POUNDS CHICKEN WINGS, CUT UP AT THE JOINTS

1 MEDIUM CARROT, PEELED AND CHOPPED

½ CELERY STALK, CHOPPED

½ LEEK, WHITE AND LIGHT GREEN PARTS ONLY, CUT IN HALF LENGTHWISE AND WASHED

4 CLOVES GARLIC

1 BAY LEAF

¼ CUP PEPPERCORNS

2 SPRIGS THYME

1 (1-INCH) PIECE KOMBU

1 CLOVE STAR ANISE

1 PIECE SALMON BACON WITH RHUBARB LACQUER (SEE PAGE 47)

TO MAKE THE TARE: Mix the miso and sake together and set aside.

RAMEN NOODLES

Ramen noodles are alkali noodles, meaning they are made with flour, water, and an alkali substance called kansui, or lye water, that can be found in bottled form in most Asian markets. We use baked soda as our source. You don't have to make your own noodles but we enjoy this.

TO MAKE THE NOODLES: Combine the baked soda and the warm water together in a medium mixing bowl. Add in the cold water. Add in the flour and stir. The flour will change color from white to a golden yellow. Form a ball with the dough and knead it vigorously for about 5 minutes. Wrap the dough and let it rest in the fridge for about 1 hour.

Roll the dough out to about ⅛-inch thickness. Fold the dough into thirds. This will create a longer noodle with a smaller slice of the knife. Slice thinly to create the noodles. Toss the noodles in flour to keep them from sticking.

Heat a large pot of water to boiling. Add in a small handful of salt. Reduce to a rapid simmer and drop the noodles in the water a handful at a time. Simmer for about 2 to 3 minutes. Remove the noodles with a mesh strainer.

TO MAKE THE BROTH: Stick the cloves into the onion. Place it and the chicken wings, carrot, celery, leek, garlic, bay leaf, peppercorns, and thyme into a large stockpot. Cover with 6 cups of water. Bring the mixture to a boil, then lower the heat and simmer for an hour.

Skim any protein that accumulates on the surface periodically. Strain the broth through a fine mesh strainer and return to the stockpot.

Place the kombu, star anise clove, and a 2-inch piece of salmon bacon into the broth. Simmer for 5 minutes. Hold the broth hot for final plating.

For the Vegetables

2 TABLESPOONS CANOLA OIL

I TABLESPOON UNSALTED BUTTER

I CARROT, PEELED AND SLICED
INTO ¼-INCH SLICES

I STOCK BROCCOLINI, CUT INTO
BITE-SIZED PIECES

I CELERY STALK, WASHED AND
SLICED

12 SHIITAKE MUSHROOMS, SLICED

SALT AND FRESHLY GROUND
BLACK PEPPER

I TEASPOON LIGHT SESAME OIL

I BUNCH CILANTRO, STEMMED

2 GREEN ONIONS, SLICED

2 RED RADISHES, SLICED

For the Salmon

6 (6-OUNCE) FILLETS RED SALMON,
SKINNED AND BONED

SALT AND FRESHLY GROUND
BLACK PEPPER

CANOLA OIL

TO MAKE THE VEGETABLES: Heat the canola oil and butter in a medium sauté pan over medium-high heat. When the oil is hot, add in the carrot and the broccolini and sauté for 5 minutes.

Add in the celery and mushrooms. Sauté for an additional 5 minutes. Season with salt and pepper to taste. Stir in the sesame oil. Toss in the cilantro, green onions, and radishes to the cooked vegetables. Keep the vegetable mixture covered and warm while you prepare the salmon.

TO MAKE THE SALMON: Preheat the oven to 350°F.

Rinse the salmon and pat it completely dry. Season the salmon with salt and pepper to taste. Pan-sear the salmon in a small amount of the canola oil, presentation-side down first, until a light brown crust forms.

Place the pan in the oven until the salmon is cooked through, about 4 to 5 minutes. Once removed from the oven, using a fish spatula, carefully turn the salmon over to the presentation side.

TO ASSEMBLE: Add a small ball of tare to the bottom of 6 deep-sided, 32-ounce ramen bowls. Add I cup of the noodles to each of the bowls. Add ¼ cup of vegetables to each bowl. Pour over some of the piping hot broth into each bowl. Set a piece of salmon onto the top of the vegetables in each bowl. Serve hot.

Makes 6 servings.

SALMON MASALA

This is comfort food for a rainy day at the lodge. Our version of the popular British-Indian chicken masala, we see this dish as a metaphor for cultures merging together.

For the Masala Sauce

6 TABLESPOONS CANOLA OIL, DIVIDED

1 MEDIUM YELLOW ONION, PEELED, HALVED, AND SLICED

1 POBLANO CHILE, SEEDED, STEMMED, AND DICED

2 TEASPOONS CUMIN SEEDS

½ TEASPOON GROUND CARDAMOM

2 TEASPOONS HOMEMADE CURRY POWDER (SEE PAGE 213)

2 CLOVES GARLIC, PEELED AND MINCED

2 MEDIUM TOMATOES, GRATED ON A MEDIUM SETTING OF A BOX GRATER, SKINS DISCARDED

1 (1-INCH) KNOB OF GINGER, PEELED AND CHOPPED

SALT AND FRESHLY GROUND BLACK PEPPER

¼ CUP CHOPPED CILANTRO

1 TABLESPOON FRESH LIME JUICE

1 CUP STORE-BOUGHT OR HOME-MADE ONE-HOUR CHICKEN STOCK (SEE PAGE 60)

½ CUP STORE-BOUGHT PLAIN YOGURT OR FRESH HONEY YOGURT (SEE PAGE 211)

1 BAY LEAF

1 CINNAMON STICK

For the Salmon and to Serve

4 (6-OUNCE) FILLETS RED SALMON, SKINNED AND BONED

SALT AND PEPPER

2 TABLESPOONS CANOLA OIL

4 CUPS COOKED BASMATI RICE

4 SMALL LIME WEDGES

TO MAKE THE SAUCE: Heat 3 tablespoons of the oil in a medium sauté pan over medium high heat. Stir in the onions and chile and cook until they are browned. Add in the cumin, cardamom, curry powder, garlic, tomato, and ginger. Add in an additional 3 tablespoons of oil. Season the spice mixture with salt and pepper. Cook until the spices are just aromatic.

In food processor, pulse together the onion mixture, cilantro, and the lime juice. Blend until the mixture is smooth. Return the mixture to the pan over medium heat. Add in the stock, yogurt, bay leaf, and cinnamon stick. Simmer on low while you cook the salmon.

TO MAKE THE SALMON:

Preheat the oven to 350°F.

Rinse the salmon fillets under cold water and pat them dry. Season the fillets with salt and pepper to taste. Heat the canola oil in a medium sauté pan. Place the fillets in the pan, presentation-side down. Sear the salmon until it has a brown crust. Place the pan in the oven until the salmon is cooked through, about 4 to 5 minutes.

To serve: Remove the salmon from the oven and place it over the rice. Scoop ladles of the masala sauce over the salmon. Serve with slices of lime.

Makes 4 servings.

WHITE BEAN STEW

This is what we think a French cassoulet might be. We know our French guests love this Alaska version. Serve this white bean stew with hot crusty bread.

1 POUND DRIED GREAT NORTHERN BEANS, RINSED AND PICKED THROUGH

5 OUNCES MEXICAN-STYLE CHORIZO

1 TABLESPOON TOMATO PASTE

2 MEDIUM CARROTS, DICED

1 YELLOW ONION, DICED

3 CLOVES GARLIC, MINCED

SALT AND FRESHLY GROUND BLACK PEPPER

1 (14-OUNCE) CAN CRUSHED TOMATOES

8 CUPS STORE-BOUGHT OR HOME-MADE ONE-HOUR CHICKEN STOCK (SEE PAGE 60)

4 ALASKA SEAFOOD SAUSAGES (SEE PAGE 184)

2 REINDEER SAUSAGES

1 SMALL BUNCH SWISS CHARD

1 TABLESPOON BALSAMIC VINEGAR

Soak the beans overnight, covered in cool water. Drain and rinse them. Set them aside.

In a heavy casserole or stockpot, sauté the chorizo over medium heat. Add in the tomato paste. Stir and cook this mixture for about a minute. Add in the carrots, onion, and garlic and turn the heat fairly low. Season with salt and pepper to taste. Cook, continuing to stir, until the vegetables have softened, about 5 minutes.

Add in the crushed tomatoes and the white beans. Cover the beans with the chicken stock. Bring the mixture to a boil, then reduce the heat and simmer for about 2 hours (depending on how old your beans are).

Heat the seafood and reindeer sausages in a sauté pan over medium heat for a couple of minutes, turning them to brown on all sides. Remove the sausages and slice them into half-inch rounds, dropping them into the simmering bean mixture.

Wash the Swiss chard well and trim the leaves away from the stems. Pat the leaves dry. Tear or cut the leaves into bite-sized pieces.

When the beans are tender to the bite, turn down the heat to the lowest setting. Taste a bit of the liquid and add any additional salt if needed. Stir in the Swiss chard. The heat of the beans will wilt and cook the chard in only a minute or two.

Just before serving, remove the pot from the heat and drizzle the vinegar over the beans and stir gently. This adds a little acidic edge to the flavor of the beans.

Ladle some of the beans into warm individual serving bowls and serve with hot, crusty bread.

Makes 4 to 6 servings.

PANTRY FAVORITES

AIOLI

This delicious garlic mayonnaise is a kitchen staple used in many recipes. We prefer to add in a bit of black pepper but it is optional.

3 CLOVES GARLIC, PEELED AND MINCED

I TEASPOON SALT

I LARGE EGG YOLK, ROOM TEMPERATURE

JUICE OF ½ LEMON

I CUP PURE OLIVE OIL (NOT EXTRA VIRGIN)

FRESHLY GROUND BLACK PEPPER (OPTIONAL)

Place the garlic and salt into a food processor fitted with a metal blade. Pulse for 2 seconds. Add in the egg yolk and lemon juice, pulsing until the egg is frothy. Continuously running the processor, add in enough olive oil in a thin stream to make a thick mayonnaise consistency. Add in a few twists of black pepper if desired.

Makes about I cup aioli.

BRIOCHE DOUGH

We use this recipe for a variety of different breads and practically every meal (French toast, herb rolls, dinner bread). We've included instructions in this collection for doughnuts and for monkey bread. We make the dough the night before serving.

½ CUP WHOLE MILK, WARM TO THE TOUCH, ABOUT 80°F

2½ TEASPOONS (I PACKAGE) ACTIVE DRY YEAST

3 TABLESPOONS GRANULATED SUGAR

I TEASPOON SALT

3 LARGE EGGS

2 CUPS BREAD FLOUR

¾ CUP (1½ STICKS) UNSALTED BUTTER, SOFTENED

Put the milk into the bowl of a stand mixer. Sprinkle in the yeast, sugar, and salt. Whisk the mixture together using the whisk attachment. Let the mixture sit for a few minutes. Change the mixer attachment to the dough hook and add the eggs and flour into the milk mixture. Scrape down the dough and make sure it is all mixed in. Mix the dough for about 20 minutes on medium speed. Add in the butter I tablespoon at a time.

Remove the mixing bowl from the mixer. Cover the dough with a clean towel and set it aside in a warm place to rise until doubled in size, about 2 hours. Knead the dough lightly and place it into a clean buttered bowl that is about twice the size of the dough. The dough will be loose and soft. Refrigerate overnight.

Makes I pound brioche dough.

BLUEBERRY CHUTNEY

If you are lucky enough to pick your own blueberries, don't wash them until right before use. They will stay refrigerated for up to two weeks. This chutney frequently appears on our cheese board at appetizer hour.

2 PINTS FRESH BLUEBERRIES

½ SMALL RED ONION, PEELED AND DICED

I CUP DRIED BLUEBERRIES

I CLOVE GARLIC, PEELED AND MINCED

I (½-INCH) KNOB FRESH GINGER, PEELED AND MINCED

I TEASPOON FRESHLY GRATED ORANGE PEEL

I½ CUPS PACKED BROWN SUGAR

I CUP APPLE JUICE

I CUP CIDER VINEGAR

Combine the blueberries, red onion, dried blueberries, garlic, ginger, orange peel, brown sugar, and apple juice in a large saucepan. Bring the mixture to a boil, reduce the heat, and simmer over medium-low for 30 minutes. Add in the vinegar. Continue to cook over medium-low heat until the mixture is thickened, about 20 additional minutes.

Makes I½ quarts chutney.

CLARIFIED BUTTER

Clarified butter, called ghee in Indian cuisine, is a handy pantry item to have on hand.

Melt ½ cup (1 stick) of butter in a small saucepan over low heat. Let it froth and bubble for 7 to 10 minutes. The milk solids will begin to caramelize in the bottom of the pan.

While the butter is melting, fill a large mixing bowl about halfway with cold water.

Plunge the saucepan in the bowl of cold water to immediately cool it down. Pour off the clarified butter into a small bowl, leaving the milky solids in the bottom of the pan. The solids can be discarded or saved as a simple spread for morning toast.

Makes 6 tablespoons clarified butter.

CRABAPPLE CHUTNEY

We have quite a few crabapple trees, which have all been planted and are not native, but we appreciate them all the same. This is a last-guests-of-the-summer recipe we make in September.

2 POUNDS CRABAPPLES, CORED
  AND CHOPPED

2 MEDIUM RED ONIONS, PEELED
  AND DICED

1 CLOVE GARLIC, PEELED AND
  MINCED

1 (1-INCH) KNOB GINGER, PEELED
  AND GRATED

2 THAI BIRD CHILES

1½ CUPS PACKED BROWN SUGAR

1 STAR ANISE, BROKEN

2 TEASPOONS SALT

⅔ CUP APPLE CIDER VINEGAR

ZEST AND JUICE OF 2 LEMONS

1 CUP GOLDEN RAISINS

APPLE JUICE

Put the crabapples, onion, garlic, ginger, chiles, brown sugar, star anise, salt, vinegar, lemon zest, lemon juice, and raisins into a large heavy-bottomed stockpot. Simmer on low heat for about 30 minutes. Adjust for the thickness by adding in any apple juice if necessary.

Makes 4 cups chutney.

FENNEL RÉMOULADE

This is a light and flavorful topping we use on our rosti crab cakes, but it is great on halibut and salmon as well.

For the Fennel Rémoulade

3 TABLESPOONS MAYONNAISE

3 TABLESPOONS LEMON JUICE

2 TABLESPOONS DIJON MUSTARD

2 SHALLOTS, CHOPPED

2 TABLESPOONS CHOPPED
  PARSLEY

2 TABLESPOONS CHOPPED
  TARRAGON

1 TEASPOON CAPERS

1 SMALL FENNEL BULB, TRIMMED,
  QUARTERED, AND SLICED THINLY

SALT AND FRESHLY GROUND BLACK
  PEPPER

Mix the mayonnaise, lemon juice, and mustard together in a large mixing bowl. Stir in the shallots, parsley, tarragon, and capers. Add in the fennel and mix. Season with salt and pepper to taste.

Cover and refrigerate at least 1 hour, or until chilled. Serve cold.

Makes 1 cup rémoulade sauce.

FRESH HONEY YOGURT

We like to use organic milk and yogurt starters to create an impeccable product. We use mild Alaska honey that adds a hint of sweetness. If you like thick Greek-style yogurt, strain the final product through moistened cheesecloth to thicken.

For the Fresh Honey Yogurt

1 QUART WHOLE MILK

¼ CUP PLAIN UNSWEETENED YOGURT

1 TABLESPOON HONEY

Clean a 1-quart wide-mouth jar with a lid and ring by running them through a sanitizing dishwashing cycle or by boiling them for a minute or two in a water bath.

Heat the milk in a large saucepan. Use an instant-read thermometer until the milk reaches 180°F. Remove the milk from the heat.

When the temperature drops to 110°F (don't go below this), stir in the yogurt and the honey, and then pour the mixture into the jar. Cover it with the lid and ring.

The yogurt needs to be in a warm place (ideally between 105-112°F) for about a day. We like to put the jars of yogurt on the shelf above our stove wrapped in cotton kitchen cloth to keep warm, but find any warm place to store the yogurt where it can be undisturbed. Some people use heating pads or ice chests filled with warm water.

After the incubation period, chill the yogurt for a couple of hours and serve with homemade granola and fresh fruit. The yogurt will last for about a week in the refrigerator.

Makes 1 quart yogurt.

FRESH RICOTTA CHEESE

Making quick cheese in our kitchen is a three-decade tradition. Homemade ricotta is much less grainy than commercially available cheese. You can substitute heavy cream for the buttermilk and lemon juice for the vinegar.

2 QUARTS WHOLE MILK

1 CUP BUTTERMILK

3 TABLESPOONS WHITE VINEGAR

½ TEASPOON SALT

Combine the milk and buttermilk in a large heavy-bottomed saucepan set over medium-high heat. Simmer the milk mixture, stirring occasionally to prevent any scorching. Heat until a thermometer reads 185°F. This should take about 10 minutes.

Remove the pan from the heat. Add the vinegar and gently stir for 30 seconds. The milk will immediately begin separating into curds. Add the salt and continue stirring for 30 seconds longer. Let the curds sit for a few minutes.

In the meantime, place moistened cheesecloth over a strainer. If you are using exceptionally thin cheesecloth, use a double layer. Place the strainer over a bowl large enough to fit the strainer comfortably. Pour the curds and whey mixture into the strainer. Bring up the edges of the cheesecloth and fasten or tie them together. Let the mixture drain for 30 to 60 minutes. The cheese should be thick and the liquids should be separated into the bowl below the strainer. The longer you drain the cheese, the dryer and thicker it will be.

Transfer the cheese to a clean container and chill. Discard the liquid.

Makes 3½ cups ricotta.

HOMEMADE CURRY POWDER

We prefer to make our own curry spice blend. Make this curry powder as spicy or mild as you prefer by adjusting the cayenne pepper.

1 TEASPOON CUMIN SEEDS

½ TEASPOON CORIANDER SEEDS

1 TEASPOON FENNEL SEEDS

½ TEASPOON MUSTARD SEED

¼ TEASPOON CLOVE

½ TEASPOON WHOLE BLACK PEPPERCORNS

¼ OF A CINNAMON STICK

1 BAY LEAF

1 TEASPOON GROUND GINGER

1 TEASPOON CAYENNE PEPPER

1 TEASPOON PAPRIKA

1 TEASPOON TURMERIC

Toast the cumin, coriander, fennel, mustard, clove, peppercorns, cinnamon, and bay leaf in a small sauté pan over medium heat until the spices are aromatic.

Grind the toasted spices in a small spice or coffee grinder.

Combine the toasted spices with the ginger, cayenne pepper, paprika, and turmeric.

Store the curry powder in a small tightly sealed container away from heat or light. The spice blend is good for about 2 months.

Makes 3 tablespoons curry powder.

PASTA DOUGH

This is our all-purpose pasta recipe we use for many different types of dishes. We prefer fresh pasta over dried for many of our recipes.

2 CUPS ALL-PURPOSE FLOUR

6 LARGE EGG YOLKS

1 WHOLE EGG

1½ TEASPOONS PURE OLIVE OIL

1 TABLESPOON MILK (A LITTLE MORE IF THE DOUGH IS DRY)

PINCH OF SALT

Place the flour onto a clean dry surface. Make a well in the center of the flour. Add in the egg yolks, whole egg, olive oil, milk, and salt.

Use your fingers to begin to combine the flour and egg mixture. At first it might not feel like the dough will come together. Just keep mixing with your fingers. (Or you can drop the whole lot into a food processor.) The dough will eventually come together into a ball. Brush aside any shaggy bits of dough that are left behind and add a little flour to your table surface as necessary.

Knead the dough until it is smooth and shiny, about 10 minutes. Use a knife or bench scraper to cut the ball of dough into several pieces. Let these rest for about 30 minutes at room temperature covered in plastic wrap so they will gain a little elasticity.

Take one piece of the dough and roll it out onto the floured surface with a rolling pin until it forms a rectangular piece about ¼ inch thick. Either continue to hand-roll the pasta with a rolling pin or use a pasta roller to continue to thin the dough to ⅛-inch thickness. Cut the dough into desired shapes.

Note that the cooking time varies for different shapes of pasta, but make sure you have plenty of well-salted simmering water to cook the pasta in. If there isn't enough volume of water, the pasta might stick to itself. Fresh pasta cooks quickly—usually within a couple of minutes—so watch it closely. You want the cooked pasta to be tender to the bite (al dente).

Makes 1 pound pasta dough.

PICKLED RED ONION

This is handy for many uses—garnish on appetizers, in salads, soups, and on our fish tacos. The longer the onions pickle, the more flavorful they become.

2 LARGE RED ONIONS

1½ CUPS APPLE CIDER VINEGAR

½ CUP GRANULATED SUGAR

Peel the onions and cut off the bottom and tops. Cut the red onion in half lengthwise, and then slice the halves into ⅛-inch-thick slices. Place the onions in either a small glass bowl or canning jar.

Heat the vinegar and sugar together in a small saucepan until the sugar has dissolved. Pour the hot liquid over the onions. Let the mixture cool to room temperature, cover, and refrigerate up to one month.

Makes about 4 cups pickled onions.

PIZZA DOUGH

We add a touch of rye flour into our pizza dough for a little added texture.

2 CUPS BREAD FLOUR, DIVIDED

2½ TEASPOONS ACTIVE DRY YEAST

2 TEASPOONS GRANULATED SUGAR

¾ TEASPOON SALT

⅔ CUP WARM WATER

1 TABLESPOON PURE OLIVE OIL

2 TABLESPOONS RYE FLOUR

In a stand mixer with the dough hook attachment, combine 1 cup of the bread flour with the yeast, sugar, and salt. With the mixer on low, add in the warm water and the oil.

Slowly add in an additional ½ cup of the bread flour and the rye flour until the dough becomes smooth. Knead with the mixer on medium-low for about 4 to 5 minutes.

Turn the mixer off and turn the dough out onto a lightly floured work surface. Add any remaining bread flour to the dough as necessary to prevent the dough from being too sticky and finish kneading it by hand. Let the dough rest at room temperature for about 15 minutes, covered. It is ready to use or can be placed covered for up to 3 days in the refrigerator.

Makes 1 pound pizza dough.

SIMPLE SALSA

This is our all-purpose salsa. We make it nearly every day when fresh tomatoes are availabl

½ RED ONION, PEELED AND DICED

2 ROMA TOMATOES, SEEDED AND
  DICED

¼ CUP CILANTRO, STEMMED AND
  CHOPPED

JUICE OF 1 LIME

ZEST OF 1 LIME

¼ TEASPOON SALT

Combine the red onion, tomatoes, cilantro, juice and zest of 1 lime, and salt in a small mixing bowl. Refrigerate until needed.

SWEET AND SMOKY SALMON RUB

This is one of many spice mixtures we use for salmon on the grill.

¼ CUP SALT

¼ CUP FIRMLY PACKED BROWN
  SUGAR

2 TABLESPOONS SMOKED PAPRIKA

2 TABLESPOONS GRANULATED
  SUGAR

1 TEASPOON GRANULATED
  GARLIC

2 TEASPOONS FRESHLY GROUND BLACK
  PEPPER

1 TEASPOON DRY MUSTARD

1 TEASPOON GROUND CUMIN

1 TEASPOON GROUND GINGER

1 TEASPOON GRATED FRESH
  ORANGE PEEL

Combine the salt, brown sugar, paprika, granulated sugar, garlic, pepper, mustard, cumin, ginger, and orange peel. Rub the spice mixture onto a salmon fillet 10 minutes before cooking. This rub will stay good for 3 months stored in an airtight container.

Makes 1 cup rub.

INDEX

ABOUT THE AUTHORS
Kirsten Dixon and Mandy Dixon

A passionate culinary student and educator, chef Kirsten Dixon has been cooking in the backcountry of Alaska for more than twenty years. She owns Within the Wild Adventure Company along with her husband, Carl, and daughters, Mandy and Carly. Together they operate Winterlake Lodge, Tutka Bay Lodge, the Cooking School at Tutka Bay, a home goods boutique, and a café, all located in Southcentral Alaska.

Kirsten completed a Master of Fine Arts program in creative writing at Goddard College, Vermont, and has since written for and been featured in many national and international publications. She has written two cookbooks, including *The Winterlake Lodge Cookbook* for which she won the Best Female Chef USA award at the Gourmand International Cookbook Awards in 2004. Her new edition of *The Winterlake Lodge Cookbook* with new recipes, new design, and new photos was published in 2012.

Mandy Dixon serves as Within the Wild Adventure Company's pastry chef and the chef of La Baleine Café, a seaside cafe in Homer, Alaska. She trained at Le Cordon Bleu in Pasadena, California, and later enrolled in the intensive pastry program at the Culinary Institute of America in St. Helena, California. Mandy worked as a pastry chef for the Thomas Keller Restaurant Group in Yountville, California, before returning to the family business in Alaska in 2010. She was the food stylist for the second edition of *The Winterlake Lodge Cookbook*.